Autistic Thinking

HOW AUTISTIC BRAINS THINK, LEARN & REMEMBER

ALONDRA ROGERS, DSW, LMSW

Text copyright © 2024 by Alondra Rogers

All rights reserved. Published in the United States by Divergent Autism Services, LLC, Portland, Oregon.

Visit us at: www.DivergentAutismServices.com

Library of Congress Cataloging-in-Publication Data
Names: Rogers, Alondra, author.
Title: Autistic Thinking: How Autistic Brains Think, Learn and Remember /
Alondra Rogers
Description: First edition | Portland: Divergent Autism Services, [2024] | Audience: Ages 14+ | Audience: Grades 10-12. | Summary: Non-fiction guide to understanding Autistic thinking.
Identifiers: LCCN *pending* (print) | ISNB 979-8-870-55113-5
Subjects: Autism. Cognition. Psychology.

The text of this book is set in 12-point Book Antiqua
Cover, interior design, and typos by the author.

Printed in the United States

For my Autistic "siblings," who are learning to love themselves and laboring for understanding and acceptance. For the misfits and weirdos of the past who never had the chance to know they were fish judged on their ability to climb trees. For all of the Autistics who have been misunderstood, marginalized, and silenced yet still dream. May this book honor your experiences, celebrate your differences, and help pave the way for a more inclusive and accepting world for all of us.

For my misfit grandmother and my Autistic daughter.

Table of Contents

Introduction
Page 11

Chapter 1: The Autistic Brain as a Unique Web: How Under- and Over- Connectedness Direct Autistic Thinking
Page 25

Chapter 2: The Whole is Greater Than the Sum of Its Parts: Autistics Need to See the "Big Picture" — and Know the "Why"
Page 55

Chapter 3: Thinking in Patterns: How Autistic People Think in Images, Words, Schematics, or the Nebulous "Other"
Page 87

Chapter 4: Comfort in Sameness: Monotropism, Interest-Based Attention, and Learning
Page 115

Chapter 5: Executive Functioning: Adulting and Other Misadventures
Page 133

Chapter 6: Autism and Memory: Wait, What Were We Talking About?
Page 163

Afterword
Page 192

Appendices
Page 194

Introduction

For most of the past 40 years, medical and educational communities have approached Autistic thinking and learning as if Autistic* people learn and think like neurotypical people, only more slowly. The usual approach to teaching Autistic people information, concepts, and skills is to slow down the process, break it into smaller pieces, and add lots of repetition.

Though Autistic people may process new information at a different speed — sometimes faster, sometimes slower — this isn't usually how they learn. Autistic brains don't function like neurotypical brains. Functional MRIs mapping the connections of typical and Autistic brains find that while typical brains all look similar to one another, Autistic brains not only look different from typical controls, but they also look different from one another.[1]

While classrooms emphasize token economies and lessons with bite-sized information and super-sized repetition, Autistic kids, overwhelmed by the social and sensory aspects of school, can get bored and confused when information is disjointed and disconnected from meaning. We could do

---

* Throughout this book, I will use Identity-First language and neurodiversity-affirming language as much as possible. Please see the Appendix for information on the history of language in the disability movement.

[1] Hahamy A, Behrmann M, Malach R. The idiosyncratic brain: distortion of spontaneous connectivity patterns in autism spectrum disorder. Nature Neuroscience. 2015 Feb;18(2):302-9. https://doi:10.1038/nn.3919

better in all settings to support Autistic children and adults if those supporting them better understood how they think.

Autistic people aren't likely to have been given information about how their brains work even if they received a professional diagnosis as either a child or an adult. Parents aren't likely to have been given much information about Autism when their child was diagnosed. And, depending on their discipline, professionals may have received very little or even no information in their education or training programs on Autism. As an adult therapist-in-training in my social work program, I received none. Those who did may have been given information that was biased, outdated, or both. This is changing due to the advocacy of Autistic people.

Though researchers continue to learn about the Autistic brain, that information is slow to make its way to those who need it the most: Autistic people, parents and family members, the therapists and doctors who serve Autistic people, and the educators who teach them.

This book is written for my fellow Autistics. The information here is intended to help you learn how your brain works so you can move with the currents of your mind instead of trying to usher your brain into patterns it was never made to participate in. This will allow you to understand and accommodate yourself and improve your daily experience.

This book is also written for parents, caregivers, and professionals who need to better understand Autistics and how to teach and support them meaningfully.

So we're all on the same page: **Autism is a neurotype, or a type of brain. It's also a disability defined as a difference in brain structure and function that corresponds to external behaviors and internal experiences, including differences in social interactions, communication, thinking, learning, and perception: it begins in fetal development and can be observed in childhood though many adults were missed as children. These differences vary among Autistics, as does the level of support needed. This definition includes those who are professionally- and self-identified.**

>>>Before we get into the tendencies of Autistic thinking, we must acknowledge that *Autistic brains aren't uniform and, therefore, do not all work the same way.* Here's a term we need to remember in all parts of this book and all parts of Autism: **heterogeneity**.

Heterogeneity is diversity—the quality of being made up of dissimilar or diverse components. Colloquially, we might say, "Autism is a spectrum," and this is what we mean. A spectrum condition is a group of related conditions and not just one.

While we work through these chapters, we have to keep in mind that there will be some Autistics for whom that particular approach doesn't apply. **The caveat to this book is that almost no theory can apply to each and every Autistic person.** Culture, identity, and other conditions are other factors that can and do influence thinking as well.

Intersectional Identities

Culture and identity can significantly affect thinking. They shape our beliefs, values, and assumptions, which in turn affect how we process information, perceive the world, and make decisions. Identity, including factors like race, gender, and socioeconomic status, also plays a role in shaping our thoughts and perspectives. Cultural norms and values, language and communication, cultural frameworks, socialization and upbringing, identity and belonging, power dynamics, and even how we view knowledge and truth are impacted by our cultural memberships and individual identities.

Your author is an Autistic/ADHD white, cis, heterosexual, secular, Xennial (cusp of Gen X and Millennial) woman born into poverty who is now middle class. My cultural identities influence how I see and experience the world and how I am seen and treated as well. While I endeavor to be aware and knowledgeable about the role of culture and identity, I can only ever learn from those with lived experiences of other cultures and identities. My knowledge of these experiences will always be incomplete. In this book, I try to represent common Autistic experiences, but these will also be influenced by an individual's other identities.

Other Conditions

Autistics usually have co-occurring conditions. Some of these can impact their thinking and cognitive processes. Some examples include:

1. ADHD: Attention Deficit Hyperactivity Disorder can affect executive function and processing speed, potentially influencing focus, organization, and processing of information.

2. Mental health conditions can impact thinking patterns in multiple different ways. Anxiety and depression or Bipolar and Schizophrenia have an impact on thinking that may intersect or diverge from some of the content in this book.

3. Sensory Processing (SPD): Sensory processing differences can influence how Autistic people perceive and process sensory information, potentially affecting their thinking and learning. A person in sensory overload is not able to learn calculus or shoe tying.

4. Dyslexia, Dyscalculia, and other learning disabilities: These can impact the processing of written or numerical information, potentially affecting thinking and problem-solving strategies.

5. Epilepsy or seizure disorders: Neurological conditions can influence cognitive function, potentially affecting thinking, memory, and processing speed.

6. Trauma or PTSD: Traumatic experiences can impact thinking patterns, leading to increased hypervigilance, avoidance, or intrusive thoughts, which may intersect with Autistic thinking styles and disrupt the person's thinking patterns.

7. Chronic pain: Physical conditions can impact cognitive function, potentially affecting thinking, focus, and processing speed.

8. Co-occurring medical conditions: Conditions like gastrointestinal issues or autoimmune disorders can impact cognitive function and thinking patterns.

9. Other brain differences: intellectual disabilities, traumatic brain injuries, or other congenital brain formation differences that make those brains somewhat different than most other Autistic brains.

10. Sleep Disorders: Chronic sleep issues can impact thinking, learning, and executive functions.

What is presented here is what is more common, what is currently supported by research, and what is supported by the lived experience of Autistic people, including me. Still, please keep in mind that other identities and conditions can also influence thinking, learning, and memory.

The Research

While we may like to see research as proof positive, it's always in a state of movement. Research isn't "fact;" it's science, and science changes based on new information. Science is built upon itself. We gain knowledge through studies little by little. When the research is repeated and stands up over time to the scrutiny of other researchers and the public, it becomes an accepted theory — until some new research pushes back with new information. However, research can be subject to bias because people are subject to bias. Research on Autistic people is usually conducted by non-Autistic people who have assumptions about Autism that inform how they design and interpret their studies. Many studies only recruit Autistics with low support needs. Many studies only recruit Autistics who are male. Many studies are on children only. Many studies only include those who are professionally diagnosed. That means our research is wobbly. There, I said it.

I will point to research throughout this book because it's the information we have right now, but it may change, and the research may be based on assumptions that are incorrect. I will provide footnotes throughout for those interested in reading further on the topics and the scientific support for my statements. There will be some areas where I make hypotheses about Autism that have yet to be researched thoroughly. I will identify those as my own.

I have a high degree of reverence for the scientific method, and I believe in science. However, we have to accept some element of ambiguity in research. Here's a quick example of how we may see change: we've been told since Autism was first labeled that it occurs in boys at a much higher rate. The oft-quoted is a ratio of four boys for every one girl. New research finds that it may actually be three boys for every four girls.[2] This is because the assumptions of what Autism looks like and how it may vary have changed. As with all studies, time, methods, and repetition will tell if this is correct.

More Autistic people are going into Autism research, and more studies are including the experiences of Autistic people and not just the observations of them. This is a critical

---

[2] McCrossin, R. (2022). Finding the true number of females with autistic spectrum disorder by estimating the biases in initial recognition and clinical diagnosis. *Children, 9*(2), 272. https://doi.org/10.3390/children9020272

shift. When researchers observe a lack of eye contact in Autistic subjects, for example, and assume this means a disinterest in human interaction without learning from the individual that eye contact is physically painful, the research is useless. It can lead to stigma and strategies that do not work.[3]

How to Use This Book

This book's purpose is to provide readers with information and context about how Autistic children and adults think and interpret the world so that Autistics can be accommodated. I can't address every situation and how to accommodate Autistic people. Instead, by learning how we think, learn, relate, and remember, Autistics can better advocate for themselves, and those who love or work with Autistic people can adjust their approaches. I hope you, dear reader, will question what you know about Autism and ask questions to better meet the needs of Autistic people. Autistics aren't slow or broken neurotypicals. Our Autistic brains work as intended.

At the end of each chapter, alternative theories to what I've presented will be shared when appropriate. The advantages and disadvantages of Autistic differences will also

---

[3] Hadjikhani, N., Åsberg Johnels, J., Zürcher, N. R., Lassalle, A., Guillon, Q., Hippolyte, L., ... & Gillberg, C. (2017). Look me in the eyes: constraining gaze in the eye-region provokes abnormally high subcortical activation in autism. *Scientific Reports, 7*(1), 3163. https://doi.org/10.1038/s41598-017-03378-5

be mentioned. You will also find a summary of the chapter along with key takeaway messages for Autistic people and for those who love or work with Autistic people, as well as tips for both.

Each Autistic person is an individual and must be treated as such. Get to know yourself or the Autistic people in your life and see what applies—and what doesn't.

Though I will refer to studies, this is not intended to be an academic or long-winded exercise. Interestingly, there isn't much research on many Autistic cognitive processes compared to other aspects of Autism, like causation. I expect this to change as more Autistic researchers enter the field. Some of what is in this book is observation and personal experience. This book aims to synthesize and distill what is known to make this information as useful as possible.

This book is organized to look at aspects of cognitive function:

- Associative or webbed thinking is a hyperconnected (and hypoconnected), non-linear, divergent thinking pattern.
- Gestalt Cognitive Processing is the need to see the whole and its connections to make meaning.
- Pattern-led thinking is presented in addition to the usual "visual thinking style."

- Interest-based attention and learning, including monotropism and hyperfocus.
- Executive functions and decision-making.
- Episodic and semantic memory.

All of these work together to form how Autistic people learn, think, interact with, and interpret the world.

Autistic and other neurodivergent brains are the artists, scientists, creatives, and pragmatists. Our fellow neurodivergents have used their skills to change the world in big and small ways throughout history. Our ways of thinking are helpful and even necessary to the world, but even more so to ourselves.

One more thing before we dive in —

Neurodiversity

The human brain is incredibly complex and holds many more secrets yet to be revealed about Autism and all of the human experience. Understanding the mechanisms of difference is still the domain of neuroscience. The more information we have about how Autism works, the less stigma we have to wade through. The view of Autism this book takes, and one I hope you take as well, is that Autism is a less common type of brain but that **all** brains exist within the range of normal. It's not a defect or a design. Autism includes strengths and challenges that are opposite of most neurotypical brains.[4]

This view represents a shift in the understanding of Autism that's been building for decades, which sees Autism solely as a defect under the **medical model of disability (the prevailing way we look at disability as an individual deficit that requires treatment or cure unless that's not possible, in which case, it's a tragedy).** The viewpoint of "all brains belong" suggests a **neurodiversity paradigm** of Autism based on the concept of biodiversity that says natural variation creates diversity, which allows humans to thrive.[5] Since we live with the medical model, we can integrate an understanding of all disability as natural. The neurodiversity paradigm does not erase disability. It simply accepts it as a part of what it means to be human. All humans have periods in life that require support from others, and if we live long enough, we all experience disability.

---

[4] That's the idiosyncratic brain imaging study by Hahamy, Behrman, and Malach again.

[5] Pellicano, E. (2022). Annual Research Review: Shifting from 'normal science' to neurodiversity in autism science. *Journal of Child Psychology and Psychiatry*, 63(4), 381-396. https://doi.org/10.1111/jcpp.13534

Diversity allows a species to adapt to changes. Autistic traits are a part of neurodiversity and add to the toolkit humans have to adapt, survive, and thrive. While this book is specifically for Autistic people and those who want to learn about Autistic people, these styles of thinking are more common in people with other neurodivergences as well. Those with ADHD, Bipolar, Schizophrenia, and other conditions under the umbrella of neurodivergence may have brains that process in these ways as well. Conversely, not every Autistic or neurodivergent person will relate to every one of these traits.

That's because Autistic brains are idiosyncratic and unique. This book exists to teach you about yourself or the Autistic people in your life because knowledge is the prerequisite to support. Autistics have been misunderstood and under-supported for too long.

Chapter 1

The Autistic Brain as a Unique Web: How Under- and Over- Connectedness Direct Autistic Thinking

The Autistic brain is a system like a neurotypical brain, but the details of how that system works are very different in some of the most commonly used areas. We can see this reflected in how Autistic people behave and interact, but we can also see it in brain scans.

In my field of social work, the prevailing theory of practice is called Systems Theory. **Systems Theory asks social workers (and others) to consider the person in front of them to be at the center of complex interconnected networks.** Whether you're a therapist focusing on the person's mental health, a case worker helping them with parenting issues, or a case manager solving problems with accessing care, you view all people and all problems as part of an interconnected web of systems. These can include families, communities, education systems, family courts, and more complex and less visible systems that influence everyone, like patriarchy, racism, and capitalism. I think of Autistics as systems thinkers. In fact, that's one theory of Autism: systemizing.[6] Relative to age, experience, exposure, and intelligence, we see the world as connected in systems. We see how many concepts, events, and theories intersect. However, we also have some areas where those connections are sparse — like social relationships. This mirrors how our brains are wired.

Autistics are lateral thinkers vs. linear thinkers. Autistics are Gestalt Cognitive Processors, meaning we must see the whole and its connections to understand a concept. We rely on bottom-up reviews of information and top-down comparisons to what we already know. We use a perceptual style of thinking that may be visual or pattern-based. Our memories work differently. Our executive functioning works differently, including decision-making. How we perceive others' emotions and predict how others think or feel is also different, and how we perceive our own emotions is

---

[6] van der Zee, E., & Derksen, J. J. (2021). The power of systemizing in autism. *Child Psychiatry & Human Development*, 52(2), 321-331. https://doi.org/10.1007/s10578-020-01014-4

different. In short, while the broad strokes of being human are the same, the detail strokes are all different. And as discussed in the introduction, Autistic brains are different from neurotypical brains and from each other. This leads to a great deal of variety, reinforcing the adage from Dr. Stephen Shore (modified using identity-first language): *if you've met one Autistic person, you've met one Autistic person.* [7]

Many of these styles relate to our first topic: associative or webbed thinking. **Associative thinking is a trait in which a person's thoughts, ideas, and stored memories are linked in complex webs**. In this chapter, we will discuss how Autistic brains highly connect in some areas and connect less than neurotypical brains in others. We will explore how this difference in structure and neural communication creates what we call Autism.

---

[7] Flannery, K. A., & Wisner-Carlson, R. (2020). Autism and Education. *Child and adolescent psychiatric clinics of North America*, 29(2), 319–343. https://doi.org/10.1016/j.chc.2019.12.005

Basically, all of the theories of how Autism works boil down to this: more connections or fewer connections in the brain leading to an over-/under-sensitive and an over-/under-reactive nervous system in different domains. The intense world theory (too much), the mirror neuron theory (too little), monotropism (too much and too little, which in a neurodiversity paradigm is just right!), and even the "extreme male brain" theory (too much systemizing and not enough empathy) are all about the brain, hormones, and nervous system with too many connections or too few to be typical.[8]

This is called the **Connectivity Theory of Autism.** Over decades, research has peeled back the layers of the onion to learn more about what the connections in the brain actually look like. This work was originally done the only way it could be — post-mortem analysis of brain tissue. Now, we can use painless tools on living people that are much more useful as we can see the brain *in action,* like with functional MRIs. Before the wide availability of images from functional MRIs, the prevailing theory was one of under-connectivity — that Autistics have under-connected brains.[9] The reality is more complicated than that, as we will see.

---

[8] Theories of Autism. (N.d.). Psychology Today. Retrieved from https://www.psychologytoday.com/us/basics/autism/theories-autism

[9] Just, M. A., Cherkassky, V. L., Keller, T. A., & Minshew, N. J. (2004). Cortical activation and synchronization during sentence comprehension in high-functioning autism: evidence of underconnectivity. *Brain: a journal of neurology, 127*(Pt 8), 1811–1821. https://doi.org/10.1093/brain/awh199

At present, Autism is diagnosed using behavioral assessments that include observation and analysis of history based on parent reports on observed behaviors, but Autism can also be diagnosed with a high degree of accuracy using MRI brain scans.[10] Recognizable differences in Autistic brains are observable across the lifespan.[11]

How the structure of Autistic brains differs from neurotypical brains

In this section, we are going to get a little technical and use some anatomical terms about the brain and some of the major areas where differences are detected. These terms are included for those of you interested in the neuroscience aspect, but there's not going to be a quiz or anything on this stuff. It's fine to skip these details if they don't interest you. **The gist is this: Autistic brains are connected differently than neurotypical ones.** The "what" of these differences in these parts of the brain are in *italics* on the following pages. While these regions show differences, for simplicity,

---

[10] Noura Alotaibi, Koushik Maharatna; Classification of Autism Spectrum Disorder From EEG-Based Functional Brain Connectivity Analysis. *Neural Comput* 2021; 33 (7): 1914–1941. https://doi.org/10.1162/neco_a_01394

[11] Braden, B. B., Smith, C. J., Thompson, A., Glaspy, T. K., Wood, E., Vatsa, D., Abbott, A. E., McGee, S. C., & Baxter, L. C. (2017). Executive function and functional and structural brain differences in middle-age adults with autism spectrum disorder. *Autism Research*, 10(12), 1945-1959. https://doi.org/10.1002/aur.1842

remember the issues present in Autism can also be represented by thinking about how the brain connects different regions — with many or too few links.[12] At present, the research has connected these differences in the brain specifically to the challenges of Autism, but changes in the brain also lead to the beneficial aspects of Autism as well. We will discuss these later.

Corpus Callosum: This is a bundle of neural fibers near the center of the brain that connects both of the hemispheres. Studies show smaller corpora callosum are one of the most consistent differences in Autistic brains, and *the effects of a small corpus callosum are "atypical activity, during social cognition tasks, working memory tasks, and tasks of executive function."*[13] Other studies show that the changes in this area may vary in early childhood[14] and by sex. The studies on connectivity differences between children and adolescents suggest something changes with puberty and explain why some traits can become less acute for some Autistic adults. Studies have found sex-based differences in the structures.

---

[12] Kennedy, D. P., & Adolphs, R. (2012). The social brain in psychiatric and neurological disorders. *Trends in cognitive sciences*, 16(11), 559-572. https://doi.org/10.1016/j.tics.2012.09.006

[13] Valenti, M., Pino, M.C., Mazza, M. *et al.* Abnormal Structural and Functional Connectivity of the Corpus Callosum in Autism Spectrum Disorders: a Review. *Rev Journal of Autism & Developmental Disorders* 7, 46–62 (2020). https://doi.org/10.1007/s40489-019-00176-9

[14] Nomi, J. S., & Uddin, L. Q. (2015). Developmental changes in large-scale network connectivity in autism. *NeuroImage. Clinical*, 7, 732–741. https://doi.org/10.1016/j.nicl.2015.02.024

Other studies have found that the brains of Autistics assigned female at birth have regions that are more like the brains of neurotypical male brains rather than Autistic male or non-Autistic female brains.[15]

<u>Amygdala:</u> The amygdala is a tiny structure about the size and shape of an almond. It's shown to be altered in almost every psychiatric condition, as well as in Autism. The amygdala is a part of the brain central to sensory information, emotions, especially fear, emotionally tied memories, and decision-making. It's been found to be overgrown in infants who are later found to be Autistic and also becomes smaller than average in adulthood but is variable in some Autistics having larger and others having smaller amygdalas. *The differences influence anxiety as well as social behaviors, joint attention, repetitive behaviors, and emotional regulation.*[16] [17]

---

[15] Hernandez, L. M. (2023). Sex-differential neuroanatomy in autism: a shift toward male-characteristic brain structure. *American Journal of Psychiatry*, 180(1), 8-10. https://doi.org/10.1176/appi.ajp.20220939

[16] Avino, T. A., Barger, N., Vargas, M. V., Carlson, E. L., Amaral, D. G., Bauman, M. D., & Schumann, C. M. (2018). Neuron numbers increase in the human amygdala from birth to adulthood, but not in autism. *Proceedings of the National Academy of Sciences*, 115(14), 3710-3715. https://doi.org/10.1073/pnas.1801912115

[17] Seguin, D., Pac, S., Wang, J., Nicolson, R., Martinez-Trujillo, J., & Duerden, E. G. (2021). Amygdala subnuclei development in adolescents with autism spectrum disorder: Association with social communication and repetitive behaviors. *Brain and Behavior*, 11(8), e2299. https://doi.org/10.1002/brb3.2299

Primary motor cortex[18] Somatosensory cortex[19] and cerebellum: each of these regions is involved in movement, balance, and coordination. Research also now shows that the cerebellum is involved in regulating social behavior through dopamine production[20] as well as having a role in language and fear responses.[21]

Differences in the motor and somatosensory cortex have been shown to have difficulty communicating causing fine motor issues specifically related to motor learning. Differences in the cerebellum may impact gait, eye movement, balance, coordination, as well as social cognition.[22]

---

[18] Thompson, A., Murphy, D., Dell'Acqua, F., Ecker, C., McAlonan, G., Howells, H., Baron-Cohen, S., Lai, M. C., Lombardo, M. V., & MRC AIMS Consortium, and Marco Catani (2017). Impaired Communication Between the Motor and Somatosensory Homunculus Is Associated With Poor Manual Dexterity in Autism Spectrum Disorder. *Biological psychiatry, 81*(3), 211–219. https://doi.org/10.1016/j.biopsych.2016.06.020

[19] Nebel, M. B., Joel, S. E., Muschelli, J., Barber, A. D., Caffo, B. S., Pekar, J. J., & Mostofsky, S. H. (2014). Disruption of functional organization within the primary motor cortex in children with autism. *Human brain mapping, 35*(2), 567–580. https://doi.org/10.1002/hbm.22188

[20] D'Angelo E. (2019). The cerebellum gets social. *Science (New York, N.Y.), 363*(6424), 229. https://doi.org/10.1126/science.aaw2571

[21] Schmahmann, J. D., & Caplan, D. (2006). Cognition, emotion and the cerebellum. *Brain : a journal of neurology, 129*(Pt 2), 290–292. https://doi.org/10.1093/brain/awh729

[22] Mapelli, L., Soda, T., & Prestori, F. (2022). The Cerebellar Involvement in Autism Spectrum Disorders: From the Social Brain to Mouse Models. *International Journal of Molecular Sciences, 23*(7). https://doi.org/10.3390/ijms23073894

Insular cortex: This region of the brain processes sensory information, including vestibular (sense balance and the body in space), pain, taste, and auditory information. This cortex is also involved in empathy, risk assessment, decision making, and some basic functions of the body, such as heart rate, switching between the two nervous systems, and some basic emotions. *Differences in this area of the brain can impact these areas and are noted to have an impact on social cognition and executive function as well.*[23]

Fusiform gyrus: This structure of the brain is involved in face and object recognition, reading, memory, and perception. *Differences in this region of the brain cause difficulty in the visual processing of human faces.*[24]

---

[23] Nomi, J. S., Molnar-Szakacs, I., & Uddin, L. Q. (2019). Insular function in autism: Update and future directions in neuroimaging and interventions. *Progress in neuro-psychopharmacology & biological psychiatry, 89,* 412–426. https://doi.org/10.1016/j.pnpbp.2018.10.015

[24] Pereira, J. A., Sepulveda, P., Rana, M., Montalba, C., Tejos, C., Torres, R., Sitaram, R., & Ruiz, S. (2019). Self-Regulation of the Fusiform Face Area in Autism Spectrum: A Feasibility Study With Real-Time fMRI Neurofeedback. *Frontiers in human neuroscience, 13,* 446. https://doi.org/10.3389/fnhum.2019.00446

Anterior cingulate cortex: This structure connects the cognitive prefrontal cortex with the emotional limbic region.[25] Its role is complex. *Differences in this region influence social behaviors.*[26]

Hippocampus: The hippocampus is a hub of learning and memory. *Alterations in the hippocampus cause differences in social interaction, spatial reasoning, and memory.*[27]

Basal ganglia: These structures, like many others, are responsible for numerous functions including motor functions, cognition, speech, and social interactions. Specifically, the basal ganglia play a role in coordination, sensory modulation, hand/eye coordination, planning a sequence of actions, habit learning, and inhibition control. *Differences in this part of the brain can influence these but are also known to influence repetitive behaviors.*[28]

---

[25] Stevens, F. L., Hurley, R. A., & Taber, K. H. (2011). Anterior cingulate cortex: unique role in cognition and emotion. *The Journal of neuropsychiatry and clinical neurosciences*, 23(2), 121-125.

[26] Guo, B., Chen, J., Chen, Q., Ren, K., Feng, D., Mao, H., Yao, H., Yang, J., Liu, H., Liu, Y., Jia, F., Qi, C., Hu, H., Fu, Z., Feng, G., Wang, W., & Wu, S. (2019). Anterior cingulate cortex dysfunction underlies social deficits in Shank3 mutant mice. *Nature Neuroscience*, 22(8), 1223-1234. https://doi.org/10.1038/s41593-019-0445-9

[27] Banker, S. M., Gu, X., Schiller, D., & Foss-Feig, J. H. (2021). Hippocampal contributions to social and cognitive deficits in autism spectrum disorder. *Trends in neurosciences*, 44(10), 793-807. https://doi.org/10.1176/jnp.23.2.jnp121

[28] Subramanian, K., Brandenburg, C., Orsati, F., Soghomonian, J. J., Hussman, J. P., & Blatt, G. J. (2017). Basal ganglia and autism - a translational perspective. *Autism research : official journal of the International Society for Autism Research*, 10(11), 1751-1775. https://doi.org/10.1002/aur.1837

Pre-frontal cortex: The prefrontal cortex is one of the last parts of the brain to mature. This part of the brain is the seat of personality. It's also involved in motor function, planning, working memory, social behaviors, and some aspects of speech and language. The connections between this region and other regions of the brain appear to be under-connected.[29] Other researchers found that the motor issues in this area directly relate to non-motor functions: that is the motor dysfunction results in cognitive and emotional challenges.[30] *Alterations in this region impact executive functions and motor functions.*

Thalamus: Before 2013, sensory issues weren't included in the Diagnostic and Statistical Manual of Mental Disorders (DSM). The thalamus is responsible for switchboarding signals. *In Autistic brains, the connections can be overactive, causing more sensitivity to stimuli, and the thalamus in Autistics is less selective about what it passes along, which you may recognize as not filtering out sensory information.*[31]

---

[29] Zhao, C., Lv, R., Zhang, Y., He, M., Cai, T., Sun, Q., Yan, Y., Bao, Y., Lv, Y., & Fu, B. (2021). Alterations of Prefrontal-Posterior Information Processing Patterns in Autism Spectrum Disorders. *Frontiers in Neuroscience, 15*. https://doi.org/10.3389/fnins.2021.768219

[30] Leisman, G., Melillo, R., & Melillo, T. (2023). Prefrontal functional connectivities in autism spectrum disorders: A connectopathic disorder affecting movement, interoception, and cognition. *Brain Research Bulletin, 198*, 65-76. https://doi.org/10.1016/j.brainresbull.2023.04.004

[31] Green, S. A., Hernandez, L., Bookheimer, S. Y., & Dapretto, M. (2017). Reduced modulation of thalamocortical connectivity during exposure to sensory stimuli in ASD. *Autism Research, 10*(5), 801-809. https://doi.org/10.1002/aur.1726

Language areas: Wernicke's area (laterosuperior temporal) and Broca's area (inferior frontal gyrus): These two areas manage speech and language. Wenicke's is involved in the comprehension of language, and Broca's is involved in producing language. *Alterations in connections in these areas can cause delays in speech and produce issues with grammar, such as reversing "you" and "I."*[32].

To summarize this, Autistic brains have the same parts of the brain as neurotypicals (usually), but how they interact and function is not the same. Some areas are highly connected, and others are less connected. These differences are associated with the traits of the condition.

Dendrite Pruning: More About Autistic Neural Connections

Before we move on from the structure and function of the brain, I want to touch on an important feature of Autism that might help highlight how under- and over-connectedness happens in the Autistic brain and how it impacts Autistic thinking, learning, relating, and remembering.

---

[32] Geggel, L. (2013). Language areas of the brain activate differently in autism. https://www.spectrumnews.org/news/language-areas-of-the-brain-activate-differently-in-autism/

A dendrite is a neuron branch that reaches out to other neurons to connect and pass electrochemical signals. In typical brain development, unused neurons are pruned — that is, some neurons are identified as being unused and targeted for termination, and they wither away. This process occurs throughout infancy and through adolescence.

Researchers have found in different studies both that *pruning occurs more in Autistic subjects and also that it occurs less in Autistic subjects.* You read that right. As with other findings about the Autistic brain, *both may turn out to be correct.* Because Autism is heterogeneous in pretty much every respect, this is yet another manifestation of that heterogeneity. There are plenty of recent findings supporting under-pruning, where Autistic brains may have as little as 16% of their synapses pruned, whereas neurotypical children have about 50% pruned.[33] However, still other Autistic people have over-pruning or indiscriminate pruning, which can lead to skill regression in Autistic children.[34] It's also theorized that how pruning occurs impacts what conditions a person develops. [35]

---

[33] Tang, G., Gudsnuk, K., Kuo, S. H., Cotrina, M. L., Rosoklija, G., Sosunov, A., ... & Sulzer, D. (2014). Loss of mTOR-dependent macroautophagy causes autistic-like synaptic pruning deficits. *Neuron, 83*(5), 1131-1143. https://doi.org/10.1016/j.neuron.2014.07.040

[34] Thomas, S. C., Davis, R., Karmiloff-Smith, A., Knowland, C. P., & Charman, T. (2016). The over-pruning hypothesis of autism. *Developmental Science, 19*(2), 284-305. https://doi.org/10.1111/desc.12303

[35] de Silva, P. N. (2018). Do patterns of synaptic pruning underlie psychoses, autism and ADHD? *BJPsych Advances, 24*(3), 212-217. https://doi:10.1192/bja.2017.27

Examples of Associative Thinking

In associative thinking, "One thing leads to another," but not in the way most typical brains process. A better way to conceptualize the thought may be, "On a related note" or "That reminds me." Autistic thinking is usually a non-linear web of connections that may not appear to be connected to an outside observer.

That reminds me: brainstorming sessions. Neurotypical (and Autistic) people use brainstorming to come up with innovative ideas. The process is one of association, especially in the later stages when all of the more obvious ideas have already been shared, and participants are forced to get creative.

Brainstorming is characterized as an anything-goes event where whatever ideas come are jotted down, sometimes in a list and sometimes on a big map. This is an activity that can use both linear and associative thinking processes. It's designed to get to associative ideas or those more creative and difficult-to-get-to ideas for most neurotypical, linear thinkers. Below is an example of my brainstorming for the contents of this book.

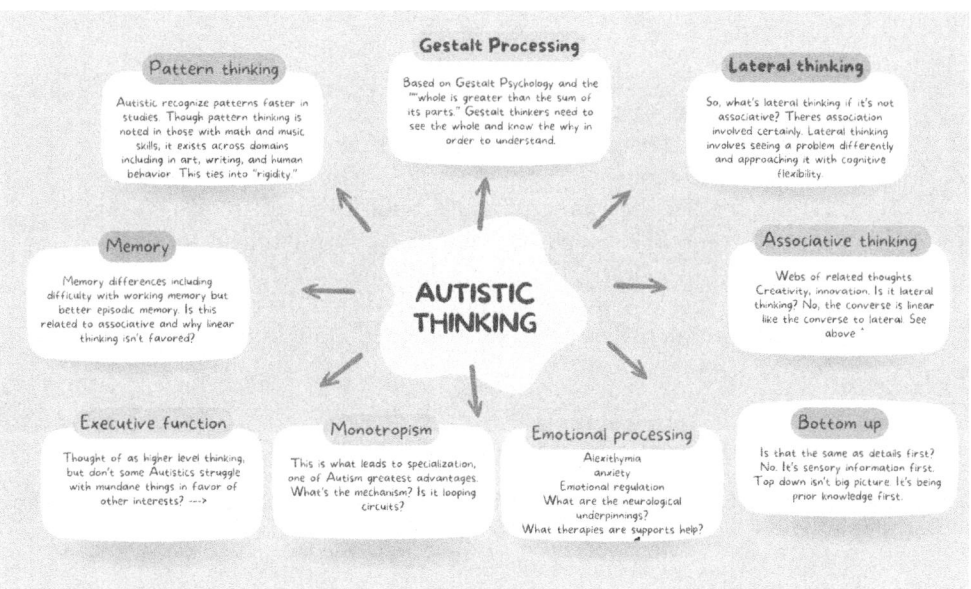

A quick brainstorm for what I wanted to include in this book. Brainstorming is probably the closest approximation of associative thinking used by neurotypical people as well as Autistics.

Temple Grandin is a well-known Autistic engineer and writer who is probably the most well-known Autistic person to the general public.[36] She writes and speaks extensively about how her brain works, including writing two books on the specific subject we will discuss later: visual thinking. She also references associative thinking when she explains how she gets from butterflies to chickens. In a 2009 essay, Grandin provides an example that involves both visual thinking and associative thinking:

---

[36] Note: Temple Grandin is also a controversial figure in the Autism community because of repeated statements that further stigmatize Autistics without spoken language or with higher support needs. Some also take issue with her support of some types of Applied Behavioral Analysis (ABA).

> If you say the word 'butterfly', the first picture I see is butterflies in my childhood backyard. The next image is metal decorative butterflies that people decorate the outside of their houses with and the third image is some butterflies I painted on a piece of plywood when I was in graduate school. Then my mind gets off the subject and I see a butterfly cut of chicken that was served at a fancy restaurant approximately 3 days ago...A teacher working with a child with autism may not understand the connection when the child suddenly switches from talking about butterflies to talking about chicken.[37]

From butterflies and chicken to football and my dad's car being in the shop. Here's an example from my life:

When I was a young, undiagnosed Autistic and ADHD kid in junior high, I remember trying to explain to a fellow student why I was "so random." I explained to a kid why, when they mentioned football, I said something about my dad's car being in the shop. The football made me think of cleats, which made me think of heels, which made me think of shoe store displays, which reminded me I needed new Purple Converse because I lost mine at the end of the year by forgetting them in my locker, which reminded me my dad was going to take me to the mall this weekend, but then I remembered that his car was in the shop.* If it wasn't ready by the weekend, I may not be able to get my shoes. Aloud, I said only the part that seemed most relevant at the time, "My dad's

---

* This run-on sentence brought to you by my brain's constant internal monologue.

[37] Grandin, T. (2009). How does visual thinking work in a person with autism? A personal account. Philosophical Transaction of the Royal Society: Biological Sciences, 364(1522). https://doi.org/10.1098/rstb.2008.0297

car is in the shop." Maybe this was only because of impulsivity, but in either case, my statements made it appear as though I hadn't listened to a thing. This experience of associating happens within seconds. It's a complex series of thoughts and images for me, but for the observer, it was me zoning off and talking about something that had nothing to do with what they were telling me about playing football this weekend.

If I were a linear thinker, I suppose I'd be thinking about football or wandering away because I have no interest in football whatsoever.

How do most people think in this respect?

Most people are linear thinkers. **<u>Linear thinking</u> is the step-by-step progression through a problem or situation.** It's usually described as logical, but I find associative thinking to be logical as well. In linear thinking, you walk through the process to an answer or a conclusion — or you don't have enough information. Not having an answer can lead to other approaches, including associated thinking. Linear thinkers can practice brainstorming and associated thinking, of course, but this isn't their natural first approach. Being able to use both is probably the most useful skill. In my experience, Autistic people don't lack the ability to solve problems linearly. **We don't always see all the steps, the same starting point, or find the linear path to be the correct one for the problem.** Autistics can often see the linear path and conclusion, but not always.

While most neurotypical people are linear thinkers, some are associative thinkers. The converse is also true—some Autistics are linear thinkers. Both of these cases are less common, however. Associative thinking is the opposite of linear thinking—so is lateral thinking—but lateral thinking and associative thinking aren't the same thing.

Autistic Hum

This seems like the perfect time to tell you about some studies on the busyness of Autistic brains. Because of our wiring, Autistics have more brain activity even at rest when compared to non-Autistic people. One study found that while at rest, Autistic people produced 42% more information.[38] This study is built upon previous studies that also show connectivity as a marker of difference.[39] (Remember the

---

[38] Pérez Velázquez, J. L., & Galán, R. F. (2013). Information gain in the brain's resting state: A new perspective on autism. *Frontiers in Neuroinformatics*, 7, 56001. https://doi.org/10.3389/fninf.2013.00037

[39] Zhou, Y., Wang, K., Liu, Y. *et al.* (2010). Spontaneous brain activity observed with functional magnetic resonance imaging as a potential biomarker in neuropsychiatric disorders. *Cognitive Neurodynamics* 4, 275–294. https://doi.org/10.1007/s11571-010-9126-9

generalizability of studies can be difficult because Autistics are all different from one another, and this study was conducted only on male subjects.)

The constant influx of information in the form of sensory data from the body, as well as the unceasing internally generated thoughts of the Autistic brain, are what I call, "Autistic hum." No matter what else is happening, the Autistic brain is always occupied. The web of connections for sensory input is never silent. Every thought and every external stimulus leads to a connection. It's never quiet in here, ya'll. This is part of the reason why processing information may take longer. This is why sensory overwhelm is easier to reach. The dial is already turned up to 10 all the time.

While I don't mean a literal hum one might hear in one's ears, I would like to draw a comparison between the Autistic hum of the constant generation of information and the story of an incessant hum that only some people hear. Or, you might say, *"That reminds me."*

Around the world, there are locations where a small percentage of people claim to hear a constant, bothersome droning.[40] Dubbed "the hum," this sound is described as a low-frequency rumble or buzzing. In some locations, the source has been found, usually machinery or an industrial site. In other places, no source can be located, and no sign of any disturbance can be measured with equipment to verify it, such as the famous Taos Hum. However, "hearers" who live in locations with the hum report a chronic state of overwhelm due to the experience.[41] It's inescapable and most bothersome in silence and when trying to sleep. Whether or not the hum is a "real thing," that is, something external to the hearer, is irrelevant to our purposes here (so are the conspiracy theories, "aliens," of course). It's real for the hearers. Like Autistics, hearers have to adjust to something ever-present that others don't experience and can't begin to understand. Autistic hum is a result of the brain's connectivity and lack of habituation to stimuli, meaning our brains don't filter excess information out as neurotypical brains do, and sometimes, that's exhausting.[42]

---

[40] Lallanilla, M. (2013). The Hum: An unexplained global phenomenon. *Live Science.* https://www.livescience.com/38427-the-hum-mystery-taos-hum.html

[41] Alexander, J. (19 May 2009). Have you heard 'The Hum?' *BBC News.* http://news.bbc.co.uk/2/hi/uk_news/8056284.stm

* [42] Jamal, W., Cardinaux, A., Haskins, A. J., Kjelgaard, M., & Sinha, P. (2021). Reduced sensory habituation in autism and its correlation with behavioral measures. *Journal of Autism and Developmental Disorders, 51,* 3153-3164. https://doi.org/10.1007/s10803-020-04780-1

Benefits of associative/webbed thinking

Associative thinking is linked to creativity and problem-solving. [43] Webbed thinking is an automatic search process the brain undertakes that involves the two types of memory: experiences (episodic) and knowledge (semantic). The difference in an Autistic brain is that stimuli can trigger branched responses that include memories and knowledge with a link to the original stimuli, even if that link isn't direct. While this can be complicated and distracting, it also leads to innovation. It's these differences that highlight how Autistic brains are wired. Literally.

Disadvantages of associative/webbed thinking

In certain contexts, parents, teachers, bosses, and others do not want innovation or solutions to problems they don't know about. They want a simple, succinct answer. Neurotypical standards can cause some social friction. Should Autistics worry about this? I'd like to say no, but it can be an issue when dealing with neurotypicals who seem inflexible in accepting alternatives, nuances, or multi-step answers.

---

[43] Beaty, R. E., & Kenett, Y. N. (2023). Associative thinking at the core of creativity. *Trends in Cognitive Sciences.* https://doi.org/10.1016/j.tics.2023.04.004

In other cases, it can make something an Autistic person wants to plan or carry out more complicated. When you can see all the steps to an action at once, it can seem too overwhelming to take on causing decision or task paralysis. However, as we will learn in the next section, being able to see the big picture is integral to understanding.

Alternative styles

Linear thinking is the alternative to associative thinking. Neurotypical people mostly have brains that function linearly. Some would also say "logically," but I do not because associative thinking still uses logic and reason. Autistic people are routinely shown to be better logical thinkers as well.[44] Linear thinking is a progressive, step-by-step approach with a sense of order. Linear thinking is associated with goal orientation. For Autistic people, the process itself is sometimes a reward.

Summary

The differences in Autistic brains aren't uniform. While one of the prevailing theories of Autism has been underconnectivity, the reality is far more complex and individual. The Connectivity Theory of Autism is supported by evidence across decades that is refined each year, finding

---

[44] Brosnan, M., Lewton, M., & Ashwin, C. (2016). Reasoning on the Autism Spectrum: A Dual Process Theory Account. *Journal of Autism and Developmental Disorders, 46*, 2115-2125. https://doi.org/10.1007/s10803-016-2742-4

that Autistic brains' tangles of connections tend to be more robust in areas where neurotypical brains are less robust and more sparse in areas where neurotypical brains are more robust. These differences help chart the traits of the condition in all of its individual iterations.

Takeaway for Autistics

Whatever route you take to making sense of problems and resolving them is perfectly fine. You aren't making things more complicated by taking a circuitous route. You're thorough, and thinking steps ahead. Sometimes, the answers will be so obvious to you that you will have a hard time backing up to explain your route. This may present a challenge for you or for others—think back to math and having to explain your answer by showing your work. In other situations with other people in your life, this will come up. Likely, you've already encountered how differently you see problems and process solutions. It's this variety of approaches that helps humans flourish. Give yourself time and grace when learning something new. The next chapter will explain more of why you need this.

Tips

1. **Understanding Your Unique Thinking Style**: Recognize that your thinking process might be different from others. Autistic brains tend to be associative, meaning thoughts, ideas, and stored concepts are linked in complex webs. Embrace this style of thinking and leverage it to your advantage in problem-solving and creativity, or at least respect the process even when it's taking you longer.

2. **Embrace Systems Thinking**: Understand that you might naturally think in terms of interconnected systems. Just like in systems theory in social work, you might see the world as interconnected networks. Recognize that this way of thinking can provide unique insights and perspectives and that this might confuse neurotypical people, too.

3. **Be Patient with Decision-Making**. Your decision-making process might differ due to your unique cognitive styles. Take your time to review information before making decisions.

4. **Understand Social Differences**: Recognize that your perception of others' emotions and social interactions might be different. Be patient with yourself in understanding social cues and predicting others' thoughts or feelings. Seek support or resources if needed.

5. **Manage Sensory Input**: Understand that your brain might process sensory information differently, leading to sensory sensitivity or overload. Find strategies to manage sensory input, such as using noise-canceling headphones or creating a sensory-friendly environment.

6. **Practice Self-Acceptance**: Embrace the diversity within yourself. Celebrate your strengths and talents while acknowledging areas where you may need support or accommodation. The goal isn't to hack yourself out of being Autistic. It's to accept who you are right now and get accommodations.

7. **Advocate for Yourself**: When you can, advocate for your needs and accommodations in various settings, whether it's at school, work, or in social situations. While it's not your responsibility to educate others about autism and promote acceptance and inclusion, having some resources to pass along can help.

8. **Find Supportive Communities**: One of the best parts about knowing you're Autistic is connecting with supportive communities of other Autistics who understand your experiences and challenges.

9. **Practice Self-Care**: Take care of your well-being by prioritizing self-care activities that help you recharge, manage stress, and avoid burnout. Find activities that bring you joy and relaxation, whether it's engaging in special interests, spending time in nature, or practicing mindfulness techniques.

Takeaway for those who love or work with Autistics

Autistic people are more likely to see how seemingly unrelated topics are related. This is important to understand for communication even with very young children who use Gestalts (echolalia, vocal repetition, or scripts, which are chunks of language to convey meaning that may not seem to apply to the current situation—it often does).

You may find yourself saying, "Why don't you just…" or "Why can't we just…" at times when you are working through a problem with an Autistic person. There's likely to be a reason they've already considered. There will be times when you may need to ask for clarification, but many times, you don't; it's ok to just let them pursue the solution they have decided upon, step back, and see where it goes along with them.

Tips

1. **Presume Competence:** Approach every interaction with an autistic individual with the assumption that they are capable and competent. Avoid underestimating their abilities based on preconceived notions or stereotypes. By presuming competence, you respect and empower Autistics.

2. **Understanding Neurodiversity**: Educate yourself about Autism from Autistic sources and recognize the unique thinking styles and sensory processing differences of Autistic people.

3. **Consider brain differences:** Behaviors and learning difficulties don't happen to ruin your day. They are based on the way the person's brain is wired.

4. **Embrace Individuality**: Celebrate the diversity within the Autistic community and understand that each person has their own strengths, challenges, and support needs. Your goal is to support them, not to make them less Autistic.

5. **Create Supportive Environments**: Foster environments that respect sensory needs, communication preferences, and learning styles. Make accommodations to ensure access to education, activities, and social interactions.

6. **Clear Communication**: Use clear, concise language and provide consistent routines and expectations to support understanding. Utilize visual aids and schedules to enhance communication and comprehension that is age-appropriate and respects abilities.

7. **Encourage Special Interests**: Support and encourage Autistic special interests, as they can serve as sources of motivation and skill development. Do not use them as rewards or punishments, as this can backfire.

8. **Unconditional Positive Regard:** Move away from the standard of reinforcing positive behaviors with praise, rewards, or preferred activities. Offer genuine positive regard no matter what. That is how to form trust with people who **can't** always comply.

9. **Flexibility, Patience, and Calm**: Be flexible and patient when supporting Autistic, especially during transitions, unexpected changes, and meltdowns. Allow extra time for processing information and provide support as needed. You are a co-regulation partner. You have to be regulated to do this justice.

10. **Promote Self-Advocacy**: Encourage Autistics to develop self-advocacy skills, empowering them to communicate their needs and preferences in various settings. **That means accepting no in all of its forms.**

11. **Inclusion and Acceptance**: Foster a culture of inclusion and acceptance, promoting understanding, empathy, and respect for all individuals regardless of neurodiversity.

Chapter 2
The Whole is Greater Than the Sum of Its Parts: Autistics Need to See the "Big Picture" —and Know the "Why"

In the 1970s and 80s, psychologists and psychiatrists attempted to explain the core features of Autism from a cognitive perspective. Two of these theories make curious explorations as an Autistic person. One is a "lack of implicit mentalizing," which is very similar to the theory known as "Theory of Mind" (ToM). Implicit mentalizing and ToM are metacognitive abilities, which is a fancy way of conceptualizing the higher-level *thinking skill of thinking about other people's thinking.*

"Implicit mentalizing" is the ability to understand the affective mental states of others or intuit another person's mental state quickly and unconsciously.[45] Theory of Mind is the ability to consciously understand and attribute mental states, such as beliefs, desires, and intentions, to oneself and others *and* to recognize that others may have different perspectives or knowledge.

---

* [45] Schuwerk, T., Jarvers, I., Vuori, M., & Sodian, B. (2016). Implicit mentalizing persists beyond early childhood and is profoundly impaired in children with autism spectrum condition. *Frontiers in psychology, 7,* 227429. https://doi.org/10.1016/j.tics.2023.04.004

The second cognitive theory of Autism I want to focus on is called the **"weak central coherence" theory, which suggests that, due to wiring, Autistic people lack the ability to see the big picture,** and this leads to the struggles people experience in being Autistic. More specifically, the weak central coherence theory states that Autistics' brains are wired in such a way that there is a bias toward local processing, which causes problems with global processing and seeing the big picture.

Uta Firth, Simon Baron-Cohen, and other big names in the world of Autism research hitched some wagons to these theories as a unifying way to explain the notable aspects of Autism, especially where Autistic people struggle. While Theory of Mind and implicit mentalizing *are* common struggles for Autistic people, they don't explain many aspects of the condition's traits. Please allow me to tell you why I believe Drs. Firth, Baron-Cohen, et al. missed a crucial point on the issue of central coherence.

We absolutely do have such a bias, but we also need that global processing to understand a concept.

When Autistic people don't get the big picture and the connections between parts or the "why," we don't understand the concept or the parts. If a neurotypical observer sees an

Autistic person *in the act of learning* about small talk, for example, it may appear to the observer that the individual is missing the big picture when, in many cases, the whole concept is unclear because they haven't found the links to the big picture—*yet*. When Autistics do get the big picture, we tend to understand the concept better than neurotypical people in many cases because we've trod more ground to get there.

For example, Autistics find small talk laborious and seemingly without purpose. We are specialists, and we are interest-driven. Unless an Autistic's interests are weather or sportsball, small talk seems like disingenuous posturing and a waste of time. Actually, weather is one of my special interests, and I do not enjoy other aspects of small talk.

Knowing that small talk for neurotypical people implicitly signals safety, establishes hierarchy, and builds "weak ties"[46] makes the exercise suddenly make sense—it has a purpose. Boom: *big picture acquired*.

This doesn't mean an Autistic person will now engage in small talk because they know the purpose, but they might do so in some situations when they may not have before. (Hello, it's me!) It's no longer a mysterious ritual that everyone seems to want to do for weird reasons of their own.

---

* [46] Friedlander, J. (2019). How small talk with almost-strangers proudly effects your happiness. Vice News. https://www.vice.com/en/article/kzmb43/how-small-talk-with-almost-strangers-profoundly-affects-your-happiness

The concept that Autism's main features are the result of Autistics failing to grasp big ideas is false. In fact, many Autistic people are Gestalt processors and bottom-up thinkers. In this chapter, we will explore each of these concepts and how those lead to being subject matter experts.

Starting From the Bottom

There's a bit of a misrepresentation in the Autism community of bottom-up thinking. The conversation usually compares top-down and bottom-up by calling top-down "big-picture first" and bottom-up "details first." This isn't exactly correct because it's meshing our interest and likelihood to see details first with this type of cognitive processing.

The definition of bottom-up processing comes from psychology. It means taking in data through the senses in real time to inform meaning.[47] In contrast, **top-down processing uses prior knowledge and experience to make meaning of the stimuli or topic in question.**[48] Humans use both of these types of processing, but Autistic humans tend to do more bottom-up processing. Actually, in some studies

---

[47] Gibson, J. J. (1966). The Senses Considered as Perceptual Systems. Boston: Houghton Mifflin.

[48] Gregory, R. (1970). *The Intelligent Eye*. London: Weidenfeld and Nicolson.

looking at social information processing, Autistics were found to have weaker — not non-existent — top-down processing.[49] I believe this is because we are highly adept at seeing patterns and deviations in those patterns, so we see the differences between the stimuli before us and the similar ones from our memory. Autistic brains may just be more adept at bottom-up.

Bottom-up processing is a cognitive exercise, but it's also a sensory one. One way to think of bottom-up thinking is the brain asking, "What am I really seeing (or hearing, smelling, etc.)?" And top-down processing asks, "Have I seen (or heard, smelled, etc.) this before?" As we discussed in Chapter 1, Autistic people tend to have differences in the wiring of the parts of the brain that govern sensory processing, and we tend to take in more sensory information at once. So, if Autistic brains are taking in all the sensory data all the time without much filtering, bottom-up processing of data — data taken through the senses first — makes the most sense.

Whereas bottom-up processing takes all the information and sorts through it, saving the filtering for last — because we don't know what information is needed and what's extraneous — top-down processing makes a comparison to previous knowledge and sets aside other data for use if needed later.

---

[49] Cook, J. L., Barbalat, G., & Blakemore, S. (2012). Top-down modulation of the perception of other people in schizophrenia and autism. *Frontiers in Human Neuroscience*, *6*, 24740. https://doi.org/10.3389/fnhum.2012.00175

Autistic people tend to be interested in some details—sometimes greatly interested—and may need to know information about certain details before proceeding to the next step, but **bottom-up thinking is really about filtering**.

So, what is a real-life example of what bottom-up and top-down processing look like? There are two ways to look at these approaches. One is simple perception. The other is a cognitive process. Let's look at both.

Top-down perception	Bottom-up perception
Seeing a dark blur out the corner of your eye and assuming it's your cat.	Seeing a dark blur out the corner of your eye and looking because you want to see what it is.

Top-down cognitive processing	Bottom-up cognitive processing
Learning the ropes a new job with skills from the last job	Learning the ropes of a new job by reading all the proceedures, rules, etc.

Details First?

So, do Autistic people focus on details first? *Yes.* We tend to rely on details, notice more details, and tend to hone in on details first.[50] It's also true that Autistic traits in people without an Autism diagnosis will predict their likelihood to hone in on details first.[51] Autistic people do have differences in visual perception and movement recognition as well.[52]

The critique of this style is that we do not zoom out from details to see the big picture. This can and does happen in the learning process, and if we aren't able to get information the way we learn, we may get stuck in the details, as they say. Most of the time, when we have all the important parts, we can see the big picture and may even become experts on that subject.

An illustration of details, big picture perception, and learning

I think of my learning process as shining a flashlight in a pitch-dark room. For this exercise, imagine I'm in a spooky

---

* [50] Dakin, S., Frith, U. (2005) Vagaries of visual perception in autism. Neuron. 2005 Nov 3;48(3):497-507. https://doi.org/10.1016/j.neuron.2005.10.018

* [51] Alink, A., & Charest, I. (2020). Clinically relevant autistic traits predict greater reliance on detail for image recognition. *Scientific Reports*, 10(1), 14239. https://doi.org/10.1038/s41598-020-70953-8

* [52] Chung, S., & Son, J. W. (2020). Visual Perception in Autism Spectrum Disorder: A Review of Neuroimaging Studies. *Soa--ch'ongsonyon chongsin uihak = Journal of child & adolescent psychiatry*, 31(3), 105-120. https://doi.org/10.5765/jkacap.200018

old museum attic — no ghosts, that's a different story — with all kinds of old things covered in white sheets that I'm bumping into in the dark. I can't find a light switch. I use my small flashlight, which only illuminates a little at a time. I focus just on what is lit by my flashlight for a moment to see if I know what I'm looking at. I don't. It's a machine, but I don't know what it does. I slowly sweep the light in one direction to see more of the object. I see a pile of yarn on top of it, as well as an old box of books in various stages of binding.

Do these objects go with it? Or were they just laid here for convenience? Now, I'm curious and confused. I sweep the light slowly in the other direction, and I understand and see more of the machine. I see a switch, but I don't want to flip it yet. I don't know what might happen. I see a word written on the side, *Draper*, and that sounds familiar. I scan down. I know this is an old machine made by Draper, and it might involve books or yarn.

I get down on the floor and peer under the machine; I see more moving parts and spy a manual tucked into a pocket. The cover is missing, and the pages are yellowed and worn. I start skimming the pages. I learn how to set it up and turn it on.

Then, someone comes into the room, takes three steps, and there's a click. They turned on an overhead light with a cord I didn't know was there. Now I back up and see the large Draper industrial loom. The person who walks in asks me what I've been doing in here for so long. "It looks like a loom," they say. "Yes, it's an 1895 Northrup Automatic Loom by the Draper Corporation. I've got some wool right here. Do you want to see if it still works?" This is what learning feels like for me.

At first, I'm in the dark, confused, and unsure how to proceed. I immerse myself in the process, and if given enough time, I learn. Sometimes more than most. And yes, sometimes I can't find the light switch. This process of getting the big picture is required for me to understand.

Holistic, Global, Big Picture, or Gestalt Thinking: By any name, Autistics need the whole thing to understand the concept

This concept is so important, and yet, we don't have a name for it. The theories referenced in the section title are close but don't really speak to this specifically. Let's work through it. This is one of those concepts that hasn't been fully fleshed out in research. These are my own thoughts informed by pioneering Speech and Language Pathologists, research, and experience on what Autistic people need to see. Here's the formula as I see it:

pertinent details + big picture + connections + the why

This is how Autistics really "get" an idea to click. With basically any topic, there will be elements that we understand right away, some that come a bit later, and certain elements we must have to make meaning of a thing. The pertinent details and connections may be specific to the person.

Here's the difference between this type of thinking and the neurotypical approach: Not understanding some key elements can render a concept meaningless to Autistics. This doesn't mean Autistics can't do an associated task, but they may not do it with interest because it doesn't have any importance, and for many Autistics, it has to matter. We also may have trouble adapting to changes in the task that arise because we don't have any context or meaning.

Time for an example! Understanding theories, learning new jobs, or finally having the why behind a social behavior can all serve as "ah-ha" moments for Autistics.

Here's an example of one fresh in my mind: at a ripe ~~old~~ middle age of … let's not talk about that, actually. *Clears throat* I mentioned small talk earlier. Recently, I read something about small talk that turned on a light for me. While reading about the purpose of small talk, I came to some interesting bits of information.

1. Small talk makes up about 1/3 of [neurotypical] conversation.[53]

2. Neurotypical people's brains "tick together" or synch up during social interactions—even small talk—known as interneural synchronization. Autistic people's brains do not.[54]

3. Finally, one of the fundamental purposes of small talk is to establish safety.[55]

While I knew about the phenomenon of interneural synchronization, I did not realize it happened so often and so quickly. This information taken together suddenly made small talk make more sense.

---

[53] Methot, J. R., Rosado-Solomon, E. H., Downes, P. E., & Gabriel, A. S. (2021). Office chitchat as a social ritual: The uplifting yet distracting effects of daily small talk at work. *Academy of Management Journal*, 64(5), 1445-1471. https://doi.org/10.5465/amj.2018.1474

[54] Salmi, J., Roine, U., Glerean, E., Lahnakoski, J., Nieminen-von Wendt, T., Tani, P., ... & Sams, M. (2013). The brains of high functioning Autistics do not synchronize with those of others. *NeuroImage: Clinical*, 3, 489-497. https://doi.org/10.1016/j.nicl.2013.10.011

[55] Coupland, J. (2003) Small Talk: Social Functions, Research on Language and Social Interaction, 36:1, 1-6, https://doi.org10.1207/S15327973RLSI3601_1

For me, and many other Autistics, small talk is a curious, unnecessary, and boring substitute for real conversation. It feels salesy and slightly manipulative. If the person I just met also repeats my name back to me within a few sentences, it feels like they just read the Cliff's Notes from *How to Win Friends and Influence People*—and it ain't working for me.

Thinking about small talk as a handshake—to show a drop of defenses and trustworthiness—makes it seem less bothersome to me and opens up a new window to things I didn't know existed. For neurotypical people, small talk is a bridge between 'stranger' and 'acquaintance' without a commitment, but it's also a chance to drop a "gate" over the bridge and no longer have to continue on with a person.

Autistic people take a different approach, which may perhaps depend on their experiences with others. Some Autistic people always keep the gate down and allow a new person in after observation and a determination of trust—from an emotional, if not also a physical distance. Other Autistics have the gate perpetually up and open and may later ask a person to get off the bridge and go home or withdraw and hope they get bored and leave on their own (or tolerate it and hope it improves). Still others may have a separate policy dependent on circumstances such as a "gate-down" approach to cis straight men because of previous negative experiences, a "gate-up" policy with other Autistics, or a "gate-down" policy for co-workers.

I made it to middle age thinking small talk was purely to avoid being authentic or discussing anything uncomfortable. The moment I saw its purpose was a revelation of the 'why' that changed everything. Let me hang on that for just a minute. I mean that I had a profound insight into something I've observed my whole life and thought was meaningless, and now I see colors I didn't know existed. That's
the power of the big picture, its connections, and the "why." It's also an example of how Autistic people can live in a neurotypical world and fail to understand aspects of it — the same is true for neurotypical people. They may see behaviors in Autistic people and not understand them.

I still don't like small talk, however. When I ask, "How are you?" I actually mean it and, believe me, I want to talk about the weather. Anything else that's meaningless, general, or anything that requires fake smiling, and *I'm out.*

While small talk may feel inauthentic, it serves the purpose of protection for those who can read and heed its code. Autistics like myself rely on a vibe check that's perhaps just as nebulous to neurotypicals. Other Autistics either don't have that or they have been pushed beyond their defenses so many times as to view the Signs of the Vibe as less meaningful.

The experience I just explained is the subject of this section. Some call this **Gestalt Cognitive Processing (GCP)**, but it has other names too. I don't think any of them fully capture this "thing." Holism, Big Picture Thinking, and Global Thinking get part of the way there. I use Gestalt Cognitive Processing because it relates directly to a concept many in Autism circles already know.

You are likely to have heard about Gestalt Language Processing (GLP) if you consume content about Autism, especially if you are in spaces with Speech and Language Pathologists (SLPs), educators, or parents. GLP is how many Autistic children learn language—in chunks of meaningful speech. GLP is explained as learning language as mainly a function of episodic memory, which is the memory of a thing as it was. **In fact, SLPs have been some of the only people to talk about this concept. I hope that changes. I first heard it from Autistic Speech Therapist Rachel Dorsey.**[56]

In addition to a relationship to episodic memory, I believe this need for the big picture also relates to pattern thinking. I find these topics to be important enough to explore on their own, and I also find them to be less understandable than explaining what GCP actually looks like.

---

* [56] Rachel Dorsey, Autistic SLP. https://dorseyslp.com/

Gestalt Language Processors find meaning in phrases associated with the *experiences* of the phrase. I'm going to restate this because it's important and a bit confusing. GLPs don't learn one word's meaning at a time. They learn chunks of phrases, and those phrases' meanings come from how they learned them. We see the results of this in echolalia and scripting in children, which is the repeating of words and phrases.

For example, a child may want to see a specific friend and remember the time their parent announced, "Jayden is here to play," as their friend arrived for a pleasant visit. They may ask for another play date by repeating "Jayden here to play" 3 months after this event instead of saying what non-GLPs might say, "I want to play with Jayden again." For decades, professionals told parents these phrases were meaningless. Of course, they aren't. They can, however, be confused with vocal stimming.

Not all GLPs have expressive communication delays that look like the above example for long and may progress through the stages of language development.[57] Some GLPs may not even realize they are such. As adults, GLPs may have an affinity for using movie quotes, song lyrics, common phrases, and well-worn personal scripts in their communication. I relate to this personally because I use quotes all the time to communicate. For example, I'm fond of the 2004

---

[57] Blanc, M., Blackwell, A., & Elias, P. (2023). Using the Natural Language Acquisition Protocol to Support Gestalt Language Development. *SIG 1 Language Learning and Education.* https://doi.org/23814764000300140072

film *Shawn of the Dead* and the line, "You've got red on you," used in the film when Shawn's pen leaks on his shirt and later to refer to zombie blood. When I say this to my husband, I'm commenting on his hard day and the frustrating monotony of existence in a post-capitalist landscape filled with daily tragedies while we all have to carry on doing little jobs and washing the dishes. It's a way to convey something complex simply. This is shorthand. However, it only works if the other person knows the context and the meaning.

Less commonly discussed or known is the relationship between Gestalt Language Processors and Gestalt Cognitive Processors. Gestalt is a school of psychology founded in the early 1900s as a response to Structuralism, which broke mental processes into the most basic elements. The founder of the Gestalt school, Max Wertheimer, believed that humans perceive by taking in the whole, not by understanding the individual parts and adding them together.[58] Gestalt psychology applies to perception. The concept is closely related to Holism, which is another school of thought in psychology that suggests that the mind be treated as a whole and that the mind's processes are linked.[59] The Gestalt principle of wholeness was applied to language learning, which gave us the name Gestalt Language Processing. This concept of processing language is transmuted to processing or thinking the "Gestalt Cognitive Processing." Thank you, SLPs.

Let's connect these dots — **Gestalt Language Processing is a big-picture way to learn to communicate. Gestalt Cognitive Processing is a big-picture way to learn other concepts.** It requires that formula I gave you above: big picture + pertinent details + connections + the why.

There are stages of Gestalt Language Processing, and I think my example demonstrates a stage of Gestalt Cognitive Processing along the way.

---

[58] Wagemans J, Feldman J, Gepshtein S, et al. (2012). **A century of Gestalt psychology in visual perception II. Conceptual and theoretical foundations**. *Psychology Bulletin*; 138(6):1218-1252. https://doi.org/10.1037/a0029334

[59] Holism (2018). In *APA Dictionary*. Retrieved from https://dictionary.apa.org/holism

This way of understanding can extend to anything: learning to do a new job, learning the culture of a new soccer team, algebra, critical literature analysis, or fixing the brakes on a 2006 Toyota Highlander.

The Absolute Need to Know the 'Why'

While Autistics can and do perform some tasks when they don't know the why, we very often require context that makes the task meaningful to understand it. That nearly always requires the 'why.' This is known as the Need for Cognition. **The Need for Cognition is defined as a personality trait that involves "a need to structure relevant situations in meaningful, integrated ways" and "a need to understand and make reasonable the experiential world."**[60]

The defining experiment way back in the 50s found that some people with a high Need for Cognition are frustrated when they don't have it and will make efforts to seek it out. The need for a 'why' may also be related to another similar personality trait known as **Intolerance of Ambiguity, which is a need to know an answer**.[61] This trait was further defined by:

---

[60] Cohen, A.R., Stotland, E., & Wolfe, D.M. (1955). "An Experimental Investigation of Need for Cognition". *Journal of Abnormal and Social Psychology.* **51** (2): 291–294. doi:10.1037/h0042761

[61] Frenkel-Brunswik, E (1949). "Intolerance of ambiguity as an emotional and perceptual personality variable". *J. Pers.* **18** (3): 108–143. doi:10.1111/j.1467-6494.1949.tb01236.x

1. Need for categorization
2. Need for certainty
3. Inability to tolerate good and bad traits in the same person
4. Black-and-white thinking
5. A preference for the familiar
6. Rejection of change
7. Quickly selecting a solution in ambiguous circumstances to manage anxiety
8. Premature closure

Sound familiar?

Neurotypicals also benefit from knowing and understanding context and reason. Autistics don't own this or any of the traits in this book. It's not as if neurotypicals don't care about the why. What separates Autistics from neurotypicals in this sense is that neurotypicals can still perform the task with little trouble, and Autistics may not. **When an Autistic person doesn't understand a concept, it can create a wall—the Need for Cognition—the 'why' can knock down that wall and lead directly to understanding and a path to mastery.**

Intolerance of Uncertainty and Black & White Thinking

Another need many Autistics have is the need for certainty. While similar to the Intolerance of Ambiguity, Intolerance of Uncertainty is a discomfort or negative response to situations that lack a relative assurance of a positive outcome. This can lead to Autistic to black-and-white thinking (also known as dichotomous thinking).

Black-and-white thinking is a cognitive pattern where individuals tend to categorize things into absolute and mutually exclusive categories without considering shades of gray or nuances. This means that Autistics who engage in black-and-white thinking might view situations, people, or ideas as either entirely good or entirely bad, with little middle ground. For example, we may see a person as good until they do something we don't like, say smoking, and then we suddenly see them as bad and don't want anything to do with them. We might assume that if a plan doesn't work out perfectly, it's a complete failure. This thinking pattern can lead to rigid expectations and a sense of certainty, but it can also limit flexibility and adaptability in a world where most things exist on a spectrum rather than in absolute categories.

This thinking pattern is common in people. It's very easy to see on social media. The judgments of people based on one thing highlight this. In addition to Autistic people being more likely to be black-and-white thinkers, so are people with depression, anxiety, PTSD, bipolar, some personality disorders, and more. We do not own this.

Big * here. Autistic people can also be great "grey thinkers." Grey thinking is intentionally engaging in critical thinking and looking at all sides. It pushes back on black-and-white thinking. This can apply to how we view ourselves or how we view big issues. We work through black-and-white thinking by challenging those thoughts with questions and avoiding absolutes.

I used to be a black-and-white thinker as well as a very concrete thinker through and through. My brain jumped to the easiest conclusions and then slapped the dust off my hands from the effort. I also dealt with the real and not the abstract. I still have some black-and-white thoughts, especially self-judgment and safety-related thoughts about people, but the greatest change in my black-and-white and concrete thinking came from my English 1B class in my second year of college: Critical Thinking and Composition with Barbara Morrison.

I had been warned that Barbara Morrison's class was hard. Our first essay was on the short story "The Blue Hotel" by Stephen Crane,[62] about a bunch of guys at a hotel in Nebraska during a Depression and a drought. I was struggling to answer the essay question about symbolism in the story. I didn't see it. My first attempt was directly addressing the content of the story. Something major happened to my thought process during what was really a very simple exchange with my professor. It didn't happen all at once, but learning to see things differently started at this exact moment:

Using what I know now as the Socratic Method, Barbara Morrison asked me a series of questions about the story that I have no recollection of now. But, during this conversation, the flashlight turned on in the dark, and I began to see that the meaning of stories is not only the words written on the page but also the context that we exist in within all of these systems I didn't see before. The next story we read was Ernest Gaines' "The Sky is Grey."[63] This story's young protagonist's pain and suffering opened the door to understanding racism, sacrifice, love, and stoicism. I remember concluding my A- paper with a sentence about the world being neither black and white but grey like the sky. I continued to take literature classes, and my whole way of thinking about the world became abstract, analytic, and grey. It impacts everything, and I now always see multiple perspectives when considering any issue. In political issues, I

---

* [62] Crane, Stephen. (1898). *The Blue Hotel and Other Stories.* New York: Washington Square Press.

* [63] Gaines, E. (1963). *The Sky is Grey.* Mankato, MN: Creative Company.

have adopted the position of always choosing the side with less power, even though I usually understand both sides.

A note about Autism, Intellectual Disabilities, and These Ways of Knowing and Learning

The majority of Autistic people are of average or above-average intelligence, so for them, it's easy to think about ways of thinking that are rather advanced.[64] But perhaps you read this chapter and said, "Wait a second. This can't apply to all Autistic people. What about those with Intellectual Disabilities?" Important and valid question, my friend.

Autistics who have Intellectual Disabilities (ID) through a co-occurring condition (Brain injuries, toxic exposure, infections, Prader-Willi Syndrome, Trisomy 21, Fetal Alcohol Syndrome, Fragile X Syndrome, and others) may still see some of their cognitive experiences represented in this book. Because of the variation in the cause of the ID, there may be a good deal of deviation from this as well. People with ID still have the same needs and wants. They are still complicated and interesting people.

---

[64] Dawson, M., Soulières, I., Ann Gernsbacher, M., & Mottron, L. (2007). The Level and Nature of Autistic Intelligence. *Psychological Science.* https://doi.org/10.1111/j.1467-9280.2007.01954.x

If you are a person with an Intellectual Disability or you are supporting a person with ID, these ways of knowing and learning may still apply — or not. You'll have to evaluate that for yourself or work with the individual to know. Always, always presume that they can learn when given the right tools and accommodations. Work towards robust communication because the only way to understand what an Autistic person knows is to hear their communication in whatever form it takes.

My daughter is Autistic and non-speaking. She has high support needs. She communicates using Augmentative and Alternative Communication methods (AAC), including pointing to letters on a letterboard to spell. She was assumed to have ID in school testing because her motor planning disorder makes controlling her body very difficult, as evidenced by the fact that she can not speak. She does not have ID. She's smarter than I am, just a little less worldly. She has listened to me read her this book. She says, "It's very similar for me, but I don't do the flashlight thing. I just see the whole thing at once."

It's also important to keep some other information in mind about ID in Autism in mind. Research states that about 30% of Autistic people have co-occurring intellectual disabilities.[65] (In the rest of the world, it's 50% likely due to

---

[65] Jensen, M., Smolen, C., & Girirajan, S. (2020). Gene discoveries in autism are biased towards comorbidity with intellectual disability. *Journal of medical genetics*, 57(9), 647–652. https://doi.org/10.1136/jmedgenet-2019-106476.

fewer diagnoses overall).[66] I think this is probably incorrect. Here's why: There are millions—yes, millions—of undiagnosed Autistic adults in this country and every other. These are individuals who were not identified as being Autistic. Perhaps they were diagnosed with ADHD. Perhaps they weren't diagnosed with anything until adulthood. Intellectual Disability (ID) is much less likely to fly under the radar. This fact alone would drastically change this statistic, but it's not the only error in understanding or computing ID in Autism. This issue likely has an impact on many statistics about Autism.

Non-speakers, like my daughter, also make up about 30% of Autistics. The percentage of ID and the percentage of non-speakers is treated as a Venn diagram that is a circle, and that's a mistake perpetrated against non-speakers by families, schools, and professionals. When given access to communication methods they can use that accommodate their motor planning disorders; many Autistic non-speakers are shown to also be of average or above average intelligence. We can't assume non-speaking ties to ID because speaking is a motor function and not one of intelligence.

---

[66] Russell, G., Mandy, W., Elliott, D., White, R., Pittwood, T., & Ford, T. (2019). Selection bias on intellectual ability in autism research: A cross-sectional review and meta-analysis. *Molecular Autism, 10.* https://doi.org/10.1186/s13229-019-0260-x

Autistics and non-Autistics with ID are not less than and deserve to be treated well. Approaches to supporting those with ID are similar to supporting Autistics. Get to know them, their needs, and their strengths, and then adapt methods to these. Always be respectful and treat people with ID as their age and not as a "mental age" suggested by doctors or school testing.[67]

Benefits of Gestalt Cognitive Processing

When you have to know so much about a topic, including the connections to other areas and the 'why,' you end up knowing much more than the average person does on a subject. This approach to needing to know means Autistic people who use this method may have a greater breadth and depth of understanding. The Autistic's ability to master subjects is greater IF they can put in the time to learn, which is generally a function of interest. We will explore that subject in **Chapter 5,** ***Comfort in Sameness*** **when we discuss interest-based attention.**

Disadvantages of Gestalt Cognitive Processing

Any person who needs to see the big picture, the connections, the context, and the 'why' can tell you exactly what the disadvantages of this learning style are: it takes longer, and it can annoy neurotypicals.

---

* [67] See appendix for more information on "mental age."

When learning something new requires *really* understanding it cover to cover, this takes more time. Time is a commodity in our culture, and that can be a problem for Autistics who are learning under neurotypical conditions. This might be a child in school where the lesson is only a day before moving on to the next component. This might impact an adult in a new job with 20 new skills to learn as soon as possible.

It also annoys the neurotypicals in the lives of Autistics, especially when they don't understand the reason for the delays or the questions. Neurotypical people tend to interpret Autistic questions as challenges. Sometimes, this is because the questions they ask reveal flaws in the design or expose ignorance on the part of the neurotypical doing the explaining. It can also be interpreted as wasting time because the 'why' isn't important in their estimation.

I once got fired from a video store job (yes, a video store! Xennial, remember?) for pointing out ways in which the policies didn't make sense by asking questions. "Insubordination."

Alternative styles

So, what are the other ways to process information and learn for non-Gestalt learners? **Constructivism and Behaviorism.**

Constructivism is when people learn from the world by building their knowledge piece by piece. It describes people who learn and master individual concepts and build on those to create a whole. It doesn't work well for those who just don't learn this way. You can see this is probably how most people learn since it's how most schooling and other methods of instruction are taught. It goes hand in hand with the other common classroom method: Behaviorism.

Behaviorism is a learning theory focused on the environment. The classic example of behavioral theory is learning to exercise caution around a stove after you've been burned touching it. Most behaviorism is also broken down to teach component parts with the use of rewards and punishments. While Autistics can and do learn no matter what method is used, these are not the most effective for Autistic learners. **Autistics are interest-based learners who aren't generally swayed by rewards or punishments unless they are valued or feared. No one learns well when they're afraid.**

Summary

There are a great many misunderstandings about Autism and the way Autistic people interact with and understand the world. Gestalt Cognitive Processing is a term I think works well to define how Autistic people tend to require the big picture, context and connections, and the 'why' to really understand a concept and apply it. This also includes the concepts of Need for Cognition and Intolerance of Ambiguity. While these are more common in Autistic people, nothing is universal. They may or may not apply to those with Intellectual disability.

Takeaway for Autistics

When you come to new information, you may need to know more than a neurotypical person to understand it because you can't tolerate too many holes in your knowledge. The topic may not make sense for you unless you understand how it fits into a larger picture and unless you know why things are the way they are.

Tips

1. **Understand Your Cognitive Style**: Does the theory of Gestalt Cognitive Processing sound like you? Do you tend to start with bottom-up processing? Focus on details first? Knowing this can help you understand yourself and explain to others what you need to learn.

2. **Seek Context and Purpose**: Autistics may benefit from understanding the "why" behind tasks or concepts. Knowing the purpose behind something can make it more meaningful and easier to understand.

3. **Look for Concrete Examples**: When learning new concepts, look for concrete examples or real-life situations to help bring abstract ideas to life. This can help make the information more tangible and easier to understand.

4. **Advocate for Accommodations**: This can be as simple as letting someone know it's helpful to know the big picture instead of breaking everything down.

5. **Persistence and Patience**: Learning may sometimes be a gradual process, akin to shining a flashlight in a dark room. Be patient with yourself, persist, and celebrate each step forward in your understanding.

Even if it takes you more time and you have to ask more questions, your way of learning is valid, and it may lead to you knowing more about the subject than most others. It might be helpful to explain to the person you are asking that you need to understand the big picture and the why in order to fully understand.

Takeaway for those who love or work with Autistics

When Autistic people slow down and focus on details you think are unimportant, remember that this is part of the process of understanding the lay of the land, how concepts connect, and how important things are by understanding why they are the way they are. Be patient, answer questions, and be honest if you don't know the answer. Autistics respect when a person doesn't know but is willing to find out. It can create issues of trust when you are proven to have misrepresented yourself by giving false information.

Tips

1. **Recognize Diverse Cognitive Styles:** Understand that Autistics may have diverse cognitive styles, including Gestalt Cognitive Processing, bottom-up, and/or top-down processing.

2. **Provide Meaningful Context:** When working with Autistics, provide meaningful context and explain the purpose behind tasks or activities. Helping them understand the "why" can enhance their engagement and motivation.

3. **Facilitate Big Picture Understanding:** Support Autistics in grasping the big picture by helping them see connections between different concepts and understand the overarching significance of what they're learning.

4. **Use Concrete Examples:** Use concrete examples or real-life situations to illustrate abstract concepts and make them more tangible. This can enhance their understanding and retention of information.

5. **Provide Accommodations and Support:** Advocate for and provide any necessary accommodations or support to meet the individual needs of Autistics. Ensure that they have the tools and resources they need to succeed. Remember that if they can, they will.

Chapter 3

Thinking in Patterns:
How Autistic People Think in Images,
Words, Schematics, or the Nebulous "Other"

People are, by nature, pattern seekers, and pattern recognition is a primary aspect of cognition and survival.[68] Humans find and make patterns in language, music, data, behavior, and just about everything else. Autistic people are not an exception but exceptional with patterns.

You may have heard that Autistic people are "visual thinkers," and Autistic people are, indeed, more likely to think in pictures and need to see things to understand them, but that's not the whole story.

Some rather famous Autistics have discussed their visual thinking styles at length. Autistic people are found to use more visual thinking in their everyday lives than non-Autistic people who tend to think more in words.[69] However,

---

[68] Eysenck, Michael W.; Keane, Mark T. (2003). Cognitive Psychology: A Student's Handbook (4th ed.). Hove; Philadelphia; New York: Taylor & Francis. ISBN 9780863775512. OCLC 894210185.

[69] Bled, C., Guillon, Q., Soulières, I., & Bouvet, L. (2021). Thinking in pictures in everyday life situations among autistic adults. *Plos one*, 16(7), e02550. https://doi.org/10.1371/journal.pone.0255039

that doesn't reflect the range of experiences of Autistic people. **Autistics are more likely to be visual thinkers, meaning thinking in images, but we are also more likely not to have any mental imagery at all—a condition called <u>aphantasia</u>.**[70]

The visual experience of Temple Grandin discussed earlier may be categorized as **<u>hyperphantasia</u> or extremely vivid and constant mental imagery**—both cases are more common in Autistic people.[71] Aphantasia is estimated to be present in about 1% of the population and 5-6% of Autistics.[72] There appears to be a similar relationship with hyperphantasia, but the research is still in its infancy. In this chapter, we will explore the common thinking styles of Autistic people, which include the range of possibilities from visual, verbal, schematic, and "other" in what may be better categorized as "thinking in patterns."

---

[70] Zeman, A. (2024). Aphantasia and hyperphantasia: exploring imagery vividness extremes. *Trends in Cognitive Sciences.*https://doi.org/10.1016/j.tics.2024.02.007

[71] Grandin, T. (2009). How does visual thinking work in the mind of a person with autism? A personal account. *Philosophical Transactions of the Royal Society B: Biological Sciences*, 364(1522), 1437-1442. https://doi.org/10.1098/rstb.2008.0297

[72] Roestorf, A., Williams, D.M. & Grainger, C. (2023). *Seeing in the Mind's Eye. A Study of Aphantasia in Relation to Episodic Memory and Future Thinking in Autistic Adults.* Stirling Autism Research. https://stirlingautismresearch.stir.ac.uk/files/2021/05/Seeing-in-the-Minds-Eye-A-Study-of-Aphantasia-in-Relation-to-Episodic-Memory-and-Future-Thinking-in-Autistic-Adults.pdf

Pattern recognition

Pattern recognition is the cognitive process of finding similarities in a set of information and/or repetition over time. This allows for predicting outcomes, which is pretty useful as a survival skill, and in situations like boring cubicle jobs, guessing when the next bus is coming, or when Taylor Swift is dropping her next album. Other examples of pattern recognition include learning the rules of a game by playing with others, comparing and finding similarities in behaviors from different people to similar situations, and finding similarities in comparing a current experience to a past one.

You might notice that when you drive on a certain highway, there is frequently a state trooper parked hidden behind an overpass, which might influence your current and future driving habits in that location. You might notice that your dog goes to the window every morning at 10 am, and shortly after, the mail arrives. You might notice that in America, the divisive rhetoric against marginalized groups increases in election years. You might notice that eating dairy products leads to an upset stomach. If you were a soldier or marine in Iraq, you may have noticed that roadside trash or depressions in the road sometimes concealed improvised explosive devices. As you can see, pattern recognition is literally everywhere.

All people think in patterns. In fact, pattern recognition isn't only a human skill. Animals are excellent at pattern recognition as well. My eldest cat knows that after my daughter goes to sleep, I sit on the couch, work for about 90 minutes, and then go to bed. After 90 minutes, if I haven't gone to bed, she starts meowing. The lament of a kitty who wants the bedtime ritual. In fact, pattern recognition is innate, which is why classical conditioning works. **Classical conditioning is a form of learning where two things are paired and become associated.** One is considered a neutral item that becomes a signal of the second item. Pavlov's famous dogs salivated at the ringing of a bell without any other cue of a coming meal because their brains recognized the pattern established by ringing a bell before food was provided.[73]

Pattern recognition in Autism

Pattern recognition is a well-researched subject in Autism. **Autistic people are better at recognizing patterns and changes in patterns than neurotypicals.** Pattern recognition is part of the tendency of Autistic brains to systemize or have a drive toward constructing systems of predictable outcomes based on input.

---

[73]Smith, G. P. (2000). Pavlov and integrative physiology. *American Journal of Physiology-Regulatory, Integrative and Comparative Physiology,* 279(3), R743-R755. https://doi.org/10.1152/ajpregu.2000.279.3.R743

A 2013 review of 26 brain imaging studies involving 357 Autistics and compared them with 370 neurotypicals looking for differences in brain activity patterns. Researchers found that areas of the brain associated with recognizing patterns—the temporal and occipital regions—show increased activity in Autistics. The studies also revealed there's less activity in frontal brain regions linked to planning and decision-making. **This heightened visual expertise suggests a reorganization of the Autistic brain, favoring visual processing, making Autistic brains wired for visual pattern-seeking.**

Another study found that visual pattern recognition can predict Autism before it's usually detected. In the study conducted in England, the team tested 82 nine-month-old infants with an older Autistic sibling by using eye tracking to determine if they could detect the odd letter out in images that looked like the figure below.

Example image from the infant pattern recognition study

The infants were tested at nine months, 15 months, and two years in the pattern test and also for traits of Autism. The study found that children who found the deviation in the patterns readily also met the criteria for Autism either at that point or later in the study. The findings show that children who met the criteria for Autism showed superior visual perception skills as young as nine months old.[74] **This tells us that perceptive skills and pattern and deviation recognition are** *a part of Autism.*

Patterns are embedded into human thinking, and they are stamped deeper in Autistic brains, which are characterized in part by repetitive thoughts and actions. In other words, *one of the defining characteristics of Autism is a preference for patterns.*

In my own life, I readily notice changes in patterns. For example, I walk into a room and immediately notice if someone has been there and what they did. If I notice a chair shifted a few inches out of place or a book in the wrong spot on the shelf, I can deduce that someone has entered the room and spent time reading. This ability lets me piece together clues and infer the person's motivations or actions. It's automatic.

---

[74] Gliga, T., Bedford, R., Charman, T., Johnson, M. H., Baron-Cohen, S., Bolton, P., ... & Tucker, L. (2015). Enhanced visual search in infancy predicts emerging autism symptoms. *Current Biology*, 25(13), 172. https://doi.org/10.1016/j.cub.2015.05.011

I've always been drawn to detectives with a keen ability to notice patterns and breaks in the patterns because I relate to this type of innate experience.

I've also experienced noticing that something is "off" with people. I once caught a fainting pregnant woman at the post office, for example, because I noticed something not right and watched her for a second longer when I saw she was going to faint. In a full post office, I was the only person watching her at that moment.

Pattern recognition abilities are also thought to be the source of many savant skills, such as those related to math or calendar calculating.[75] Savantism is an exceptional ability that is also innate. It's reported as occurring in roughly 10% of Autistics.

While it seems likely that most Autistic people tend to be visual thinkers, this is not universal because *almost nothing in Autism is universal*. Before we get into the visual, verbal, schematic, or "none of the above" conversation, let's revisit top-down and bottom-up thinking for a minute with an eye on pattern recognition.

---

[75] Mottron, L., Dawson, M., & Soulières, I. (2009). Enhanced perception in savant syndrome: patterns, structure and creativity. *Philosophical Transactions of the Royal Society B: Biological Sciences*, 364(1522), 1385-1391. https://doi.org/10.1098/rstb.2008.0333

Top-Down, Bottom-Up Remix

Pattern recognition is an interplay between top-down and bottom-up processing. Bottom-up processing, as you'll remember, is the analysis of sensory information from the environment as raw data. Top-down processing is using prior knowledge and experience to make inferences about the present situation.

Autistics may use existing knowledge to compare present situations with previous ones, ala top-down, but I posit this is a slightly different process than it is for neurotypicals. When Autistics compare two situations, they are naturally more meticulous in finding where the comparison breaks down or deviates. Where a non-Autistic person is likely to see something similar as close enough to respond similarly to another situation, the Autistic person is likely to analyze further.

Autistics are more likely to be present with sensory information and, therefore, utilize bottom-up processing more readily. This sensitivity enables Autistics to detect even subtle patterns and anomalies that non-Autistics overlook. Autistic hyperawareness of sensory input can lead to a deeper understanding of patterns and relationships, even in complex systems.

The blending of top-down and bottom-up processing is important to the distinct thinking and perception style of pattern recognition in Autistics. Autistics possess a unique skill set where certain senses are particularly acute and memory for specific events is sharp. This wiring enables Autistics to excel at recognizing patterns, driven in part by the interplay of dual processing mechanisms.

Visuals: Thinking in Images

However we feel about Temple Grandin, she is probably the most well-known Autistic person, and what she shares about Autism becomes well-trod knowledge. Grandin discusses Autistic visual thinking pretty extensively and in detail in her books *Thinking in Pictures* and *Visual Thinking*. In these books, she describes her thinking style and discusses her personal experience of thinking, remembering, and problem-solving, all of which depend almost exclusively on imagery. In part due to her visible status as a member of the Autistic community, visual thinking is well-known to be the most common cognitive style of Autistics.

Unlike neurotypicals, who may rely more on verbal processing, Autistic people frequently engage in visual thinking. Visual thinking involves the use of mental images to comprehend information, solve problems, and remember details. For many Autistics, this mode of thinking is not only natural but also highly efficient. These visual thinking Autistics may create mental images to represent concepts, ideas, and memories, allowing them to process information in a visual, spatial manner. Pattern recognition tends to be closely related to visual thinking, but pattern recognition can also apply to many other types of stimuli and thinking.

Research studies have consistently (with a few exceptions)[76] demonstrated that Autistics excel in tasks that require visual-spatial processing, such as pattern recognition, visual memory, and creative problem-solving. These findings suggest that visual thinking is not only a characteristic feature of Autism but also a valuable cognitive asset that can be leveraged to enhance learning and understanding.

For me, images are very much a part of my thinking, but I also have a running stream of narration with occasional written words appearing in my mind. The "meme-famous" example of types of mental representations is apples. The chart below demonstrates some of the ways in which people might respond to the instructions, such as "imagine an apple." These

---

[76] Zhang M, Jiao J, Hu X, et al. **Exploring the spatial working memory and visual perception in children with autism spectrum disorder and general population with high autism-like traits**. *PLOS ONE* 2020;15(7):e0235552. https://doi.org10.1371/journal.pone.0235552

Trembath D, Vivanti G, Iacono T, Dissanayake C. (2015). Accurate or assumed: visual learning in children with ASD. *Journal of Autism and Developmental Disabilities*, 45(10):3276-3287. https://doi.org10.1007/s10803-015-2488-4

Types of
Mental Imagery

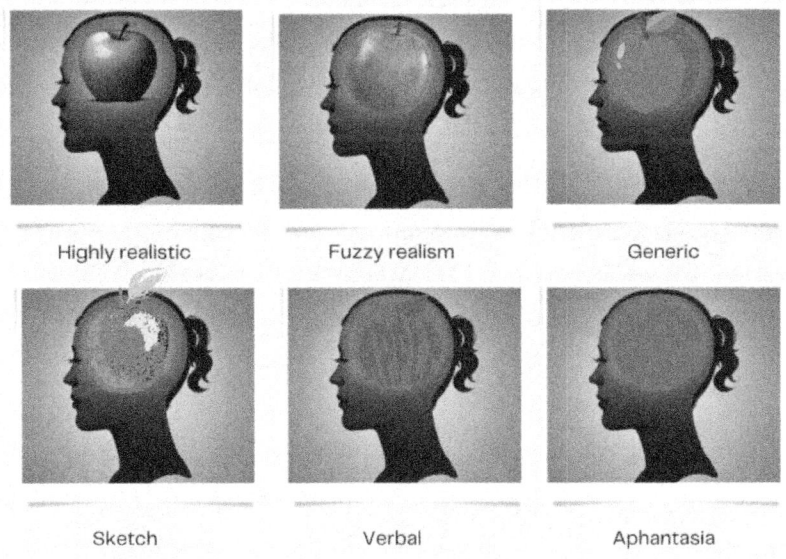

AUTISTIC THINKING
ALONDRA ROGERS, DSW, LMSW

aren't the only possibilities, but they are the most common. They include a hyper-realistic image of an actual apple, a fuzzy but still realistic apple, a generic drawn apple, a sketched version, a representation of an apple in the form of a word, no image, or something else like the concept of an apple. The images may change, and some people experience other aspects of the image, like scent, sound, or memory.

My visual images look like the "fuzzy realism." They are very much like flashbacks or dream sequences in old TV shows. They are color videos, but they are hazy. I didn't know until a few years ago that this isn't how everyone's mental images look — a Vaseline lens. I use mental imagery constantly. One example is if I'm looking for something in my home. I decide where to look for something based on a visual memory. I access an image of the object from memory and remember the last place I saw it, like a video, and then I go to that place and retrieve the item. This almost always works. There are occasions where I've remembered where the object was at a previous time and so have failed to find it. In those cases, I rely on the most likely location for something based on my habits.

The role of visual thinking in trauma

I believe there is also a dark side to a strong visual-based thinking system in Autism. It's well established that Autistic people are exposed to more traumatic events; however, Autistics are also more likely to experience events as traumatic.[77] That means that Autistic people are both more likely to be harmed by others, and they are more likely to

---

[77] Rumball, F., Happé, F., & Grey, N. (2020). Experience of trauma and PTSD symptoms in autistic adults: Risk of PTSD development following DSM-5 and non-DSM-5 traumatic life events. *Autism Research*, 13(12), 2122-2132. https://doi.org/10.1002/aur.2306

experience adverse experiences as trauma. This is attributed to the reactivity of the Autistic nervous system.[78] While this is not reflected in the literature — I can't find evidence that it's been studied yet — I suspect that the high degree of visual processing and visual memory also play a role in the effects of trauma and experiencing less significant events as traumatic. Autistic visual thinkers may hold upsetting images in memory and may construct imagery from descriptions of traumatic stories they hear from others and from media. Traumatic experiences may be stored visually as well as in the body. Autistics may also be more likely to have trauma triggers that are visual.

From my own life, I can assert that there are hundreds of images floating around in my mind that are unpleasant and triggering. A similar visual image will trigger the remembered traumatic image to resurface. This is a symptom of PTSD, intrusive thoughts or images, which can lead to another symptom, re-experiencing. These range from real traumas I

---

[78] Beauchaine, T. P., Gatzke-Kopp, L., Neuhaus, E., Chipman, J., Reid, M. J., & Webster-Stratton, C. (2013). Sympathetic- and parasympathetic-linked cardiac function and prediction of externalizing behavior, emotion regulation, and prosocial behavior among preschoolers treated for ADHD. *Journal of consulting and clinical psychology*, *81*(3), 481–493. https://doi.org/10.1037/a0032302

Fenning, R. M., Erath, S. A., Baker, J. K., Messinger, D. S., Moffitt, J., Baucom, B. R., & Kaeppler, A. K. (2019). Sympathetic-Parasympathetic Interaction and Externalizing Problems in Children with Autism Spectrum Disorder. *Autism research : official journal of the International Society for Autism Research*, *12*(12), 1805–1816. https://doi.org/10.1002/aur.2187

experienced to adverse experiences my brain has encoded as trauma to images seen in media and imagined images from traumatic tales. This is a place I'm not going to offer any examples. You deserve to be spared the same images.

Using visual thinking styles to support Autistics

In Chapter 2, we discussed the common need for Autistics to "see the big picture." Part of the need for this may be attributed to the visual thinking style most Autistics utilize. Seeing it allows for processing, understanding, and returning to the concept later through memory. The visual representation of the thing provides Autistics with the overview, the details, and maybe the why. Showing an Autistic person "what it looks like," even if the concept isn't necessarily visual, can help them make sense of it, and, *bonus,* it usually helps non-Autistic people too.

The understanding of Autistic thinking as primarily visual has led to efforts to teach Autistics with visual tools like visual schedules, pictorial communication aids, social stories, and visual reward systems. Most of these are designed by neurotypical people and don't always hit the mark to be most effective for Autistic children or adults. Part of the issue with these is that they don't address other areas of Autistic thinking or motivations. To make these tools work better for Autistics, think about including the "why" and consider motivations. Many approaches to teaching Autistic and neurotypical children rely on a system of rewards and punishments or deprivations. These aren't likely to be the most motivating. Find out what the child's intrinsic motivations are, and never use comfort items, sensory supports, or breaks as rewards. Kids should never have to work for these.

Here are some ideas for visual supports:
1. **Visual schedules for children:** I think the visual schedules used most often are helpful if used properly. Remember, routine is embedded in Autistics' brains, and knowing what to expect is crucial *when it's different than the routine*. Having the same items listed in the same order isn't that helpful when the child already knows what to expect. The most important part is when things are different. I have limited classroom experience, but from what I have seen, Autistic kids are moving items on a visual schedule to show they have done the activity, and when there's a deviation from the norm, it's not reflected on the schedule, which is when it is most important. If the weather is changing the play routine, a substitute is coming tomorrow (and this is known in advance), there's an assembly, there's a fire drill, or a class celebration, these are the times that visual schedules are helpful. Consider explaining why to the child because not knowing why can lead to being unable to accept the change, which can be a challenge in any case.

2. **Visual schedules for adults:** I use an appointment book that blocks time throughout the day. This is how I managed to get through graduate school. I blocked time for everything at the beginning of the term and wrote notes on when papers were due 1-2 weeks out. I could see the whole week and day at a glance. Other methods that work are lists and strewing. Strewing is leaving items out as no-pressure reminders. To support my executive functioning, I will leave myself items, often lined up, to do. Seeing them offers me a cue to do them. Lists with images can be helpful for some Autistics as well, but if you know they can read, it can be infantilizing to use visual schedules that we use for children, so I recommend using real images in these cases instead of the stick figure PECS cards. A photo and the word or phrase will work great.

3. **Communication aids:** Visuals can be very helpful for children and adults, but what those look like may vary from person to person, so much so that my best advice is to "try everything" and see what works best, and then *use it*. If you're a parent or a professional, respect what works and honor it. Communication is sacred.

4. **Social stories:** The concept of social stories is *chef's kiss*, but the execution is often not so great. The goal of social stories is to explain a concept and be able to tell the Autistic person what to expect. These should include things like unspoken rules, sensory aspects, and what is expected of the person. Social stories are often so basic as to be useless for the actual purpose. A social story about the sequence of events at a birthday party is helpful, but knowing that we 1. don't touch the cupcakes until after presents, 2. that there will be singing, 3. that it will be loud, and 4. you're expected to not be sad you don't get any presents is better.

5. **Social stories aren't just for kids!** Before I go to a new place, I look at the Google street view. I check out the parking situation. I read reviews. I look at the menu. Before I embark on a project, I watch a YouTuber do it first. These are also social stories. Adults can do this for themselves if able, or a care partner can assist.

6. **Visual reward systems:** These are very popular in schools and therapies. Sticker charts, checks on the board, etc. Here's the short version: these are used to inspire good behavior and curtail undesired behaviors — they don't work. These systems are based on the concept that people are in control of these behaviors, but they generally aren't. I don't want to tear down the world as we know it, but we are very much the result of the chemistry in our brains.[79] These systems are torture for Autistic kids. The offer of a reward

---

[79] Sapolsky, R. (2023). *Determined: A science of life without free will.* Penguin Press.

reads like a demand, and not reaching it feels like a punishment for having a disability. Please toss them!

Hyperphantasia

A step beyond being a visual thinker is having a mental image so vivid that it competes with the real experience. Hyperphantasia comes from the Greek word for imagination. The prefix "hyper" indicates excess. For those with hyperphantasia, internal mental imagery is as vivid as looking at an image or video in real time. For example, when a person with hyperphantasia closes their eyes, they may be able to see intricate details of objects, scenes, or events with such clarity that it feels almost as if they are actually seeing them in front of their eyes. This heightened ability to visualize can be immersive, involving multiple senses, including sight, sound, smell, taste, and touch, making the experience incredibly lifelike and rich in sensory detail. Hyperphantasia can vary in intensity among individuals, with some experiencing it more intensely than others, but overall, it provides a uniquely vivid and immersive mental imagery experience. Frankly, I'm a little jealous of this ability.

The Nebulous Other: Aphantasia

The opposite of hyperphantasia is aphantasia, which translates to "no imagination." That's an unfair definition because **aphantasia is the absence of mental imagery and not a lack of cognitive imagining**. As a person who visualizes and has a constant (incessant!) inner monologue, I am utterly fascinated by aphantasia. Aphantasia and hyperphantasia are both more common in Autistic people. The numbers I find in research don't correspond to my experience in consulting with other Autistics. It seems like there are a lot of Autistic folks out there who are Aphantasic, but as noted previously, the numbers say about 5-6%.[80]

Hearing Autistics with aphantasia discuss what their cognition is like without any imagery includes things like "my mind cycles through concepts of apples, different apples I remember seeing, the smell and texture of different kinds of apples, the waxiness of skin, biting into an apple, dipping apples in caramel, baking apple pie," "What if I can't picture an apple unless I call up memories of a specific apple?" Or " I didn't even know I couldn't imagine the thing until now."

Synesthesia

Synesthesia is a phenomenon in which stimulation of one sensory or cognitive pathway leads to automatic, involuntary experiences in another sensory pathway. Let's slow that down: **synesthesia is experiencing sensory cross-**

---

[80] Roestorf, A., Williams, D.M. & Grainger, C. (2023). *Seeing in the Mind's Eye. A Study of Aphantasia in Relation to Episodic Memory and Future Thinking in Autistic Adults.* Stirling Autism Research. https://stirlingautismresearch.stir.ac.uk/files/2021/05/Seeing-in-the-Minds-Eye-A-Study-of-Aphantasia-in-Relation-to-Episodic-Memory-and-Future-Thinking-in-Autistic-Adults.pdf

overs. This leads to a variety of different possible sensory experiences, like associating colors with numbers, seeing colors with certain words, or experiencing tastes when hearing music.

Research suggests a higher prevalence of synesthesia among Autistics compared to the general population. Impressively, almost 20% of Autistics experience synesthesia.[81] Synesthesia adds another layer of complexity to cognitive and sensory experiences, influencing how Autistics perceive and process information. Synesthesia in Autistic cognitive styles highlights the relationship between sensory processing and cognitive functioning.

For Autistic people with synesthesia, sensory stimuli can blur the lines between thinking and sensing. These heightened sensory experiences could contribute to the vividness of mental imagery and may enhance pattern recognition abilities. Of course, the sensory aspects of synesthesia may also cause sensory overload or difficulty in filtering sensory information. Thinking in images is complex and the variety within the community, from aphantasia to synesthesia, is endlessly fascinating.

---

[81] Baron-Cohen, S., Johnson, D., Asher, J., Wheelwright, S., Fisher, S. E., Gregersen, P. K., & Allison, C. (2013). Is synaesthesia more common in autism?. *Molecular autism*, 4(1), 40. https://doi.org/10.1186/2040-2392-4-40

Summary

Thinking in images is the most common manner of thinking among Autistics. This mode of cognition involves imagining mental imagery to comprehend information, solve problems, and navigate the environment. Autistics tend to excel in tasks requiring visual-spatial processing, such as pattern recognition and creative problem-solving, but it's not the only way Autistic people think. Understanding individual experience allows for the accommodating of diverse thinking styles.

Alternative styles

While the textbook says that Autistic people tend to think in imagery only, there are many ways to think. The other main method is linguistically.

Thinking in Words

Verbal thinking styles encompass the cognitive processes through which individuals primarily rely on language and words to process information, solve problems, and communicate thoughts and ideas. Unlike visual thinkers, who predominantly use mental imagery to understand concepts and navigate their surroundings, verbal thinkers excel in linguistic abilities and rely heavily on internal dialogue and verbal reasoning.

Individuals with verbal thinking styles often have a rich inner monologue, where they engage in continuous conversations with themselves to analyze situations, plan actions, and make decisions. This internal monologue is a powerful tool for problem-solving and critical thinking, allowing verbal thinkers to articulate complex ideas and formulate arguments effectively. Verbal thinkers demonstrate a strong affinity for language-based activities such as reading, writing, and verbal communication. But here's the real kicker — only about 30-50% of people have an inner monologue.[82] I have an inner monologue that is constant. I narrate everything to myself. I also see lots of imagery, but what does that mean for most people?

In neurotypical people, verbal processing often plays a dominant role in problem-solving, conceptualization, and analysis. This includes using language to understand, organize, and communicate thoughts and ideas. While imagery can also be part of neurotypical thinking, it may not always be as prominent or central as verbal processing. Imagery in neurotypical thinking often accompanies tasks

---

[82] Heavey, C. L., Moynihan, S. A., Brouwers, V. P., Lapping-Carr, L., Krumm, A. E., Kelsey, J. M., ... & Hurlburt, R. T. (2019). Measuring the frequency of inner-experience characteristics by self-report: The Nevada Inner Experience Questionnaire. *Frontiers in Psychology*, 9, 2615. https://doi.org/10.3389/fpsyg.2018.02615

such as imagining scenarios or planning for the future, but linguistic processing remains primary in many cognitive activities. But what about those moments when they aren't actively thinking about something? They are in "default mode." Yes, it's a real thing.

The Default Mode Network (DMN) is a set of cognitive and social systems in the brain that become more active when the individual isn't engaging their attention. These idling systems wander, process memories, understand the emotional states of others, and understand the self in the social context.[83] Guess what Autistic brains struggle to do? Break away from the objects of our attention, process memories, understand others, and understand our social context. The DMN is different in Autistic and other neurodivergent people, including with ADHD, depression, and schizophrenia.[84]

---

[83] Li, W., Mai, X., & Liu, C. (2014). The default mode network and social understanding of others: what do brain connectivity studies tell us. *Frontiers in human neuroscience*, 8, 74. https://doi.org/10.3389/fnhum.2014.00074

[84] Padmanabhan, A., Lynch, C. J., Schaer, M., & Menon, V. (2017). The default mode network in autism. *Biological Psychiatry: Cognitive Neuroscience and Neuroimaging*, 2(6), 476-486.https://doi.org/10.1016/j.bpsc.2017.04.004

Thinking in Schematics

Schematic thinking can be considered a subset of thinking in images depending on how it's used and involves mentally structuring information using diagrams, flowcharts, math, or music. It's characterized by the ability to break down complex concepts into simplified, structured formats, highlighting key relationships and logical sequences. Schematic thinkers excel at problem-solving by constructing mental schematics to map out potential solutions and anticipate outcomes. They rely on visual representations to clarify complex ideas and communicate them effectively. Commonly found in analytical fields like engineering and mathematics, schematic thinking offers a systematic approach to understanding and representing information, facilitating comprehension and insight into intricate systems and processes. While less prevalent than verbal or visual thinking, schematic thinking plays an important role in problem-solving and analysis, leveraging structured diagrams and flowcharts to model and design systems and structures effectively.

Benefits of Thinking in Images

Thinking in images offers several advantages, including enhanced pattern recognition, creative problem-solving, and visual memory. Autistics who think in images often excel in tasks that require visual-spatial processing, demonstrating proficiency in recognizing patterns and relationships.

Disadvantages of Thinking in Images

While visual thinking provides benefits, it can also present challenges, particularly in a language-based world and in processing traumatic imagery. Autistics with strong visual-based thinking systems may experience intrusive thoughts or images related to past traumas, leading to symptoms of PTSD and heightened sensitivity to visual triggers.

Takeaway for Autistics

While you're likely to be a visual thinker, you are certainly a pattern thinker. You may also use some other methods of thinking, such as having an inner monologue. Or, you may have no images or words in there. It's intensely valuable for you to know how you think so you can best accommodate yourself. The usual supports designed by neurotypicals may not help you—that's ok. Try something else. You beautiful brain! No matter how you think, you're pretty amazing.

Tips

Embrace Your Thinking Style: Recognize and appreciate your unique way of processing information, whether it's through visual imagery, verbal reasoning, schematic thinking, or another method. Understanding how you think can help you understand how you learn best.

Utilize Appropriate Tools: If you are a visual thinker, take advantage of visual aids to help you. These tools can provide clarity and support.

Manage Sensory Overload: Develop strategies to cope with sensory overload, especially considering your cognitive style.

Takeaway for those who love or work with Autistics

For those supporting Autistics, understanding and embracing the diversity of thinking styles is critical. Tailoring interventions to individual needs and motivations rather than relying solely on standardized approaches ensures that Autistics receive the support and accommodations necessary to thrive.

Tips

Understand Diverse Thinking Styles: Recognize that Autistic individuals may think differently from neurotypical individuals and that Autistic brains don't all think alike. There are variations in visual, verbal, and schematic thinking styles. Embrace this diversity and strive to understand each individual's unique cognitive preferences and strengths.

Provide Appropriate Supports: Gauge the thinking style of the Autistics in your life by either asking them or making observations if they aren't sure or aren't able to tell you. Adapt your approach to how they best learn. For visual learners, use visual aids such as visual schedules, communication aids, and social stories to support understanding and communication. Pair these with words to aid in identification. For verbal learners, talk through things with them. Also, be sensitive to sensory issues. When a person is overwhelmed, they may just need a break.

Foster Positive Self-Image: Promote a positive self-image and self-esteem in Autistic individuals by *authentically* celebrating their unique strengths, abilities, and accomplishments. Encourage them to embrace their neurodiversity and to feel proud of who they are. I emphasize authenticity here because Autistic people can tell when you are just giving a generic and meaningless compliment.

Be yourself: in order to build a relationship with an Autistic person, you need to be real. Kind, yes, but real. Please don't increase the volume of your voice. Please don't use "motherese," which is baby-talk to Autistic kids (and ohmygod, please do not use it with adults) when you wouldn't if the person wasn't disabled. Be yourself.

Stay Informed and Educated: Autism and Autistic culture is a dynamic subject. Stay plugged into research and Autistic spaces.

Chapter 4
Comfort in Sameness: Monotropism, Interest-Based Attention, and Learning

Yersinia Pestis, The Black Death, was an interest that consumed me beginning in the fifth grade. I asked the school librarian several times to find me more books on the Plague, and she politely referred me to the local public library. I read and re-read my school's three books on the subject, which is a pretty impressive holding for a suburban LA elementary school. That led to an interest in deadly viruses, epidemics, and apocalyptic speculation. In 10th grade, I plowed through Stephen King's *The Stand*, and in 12th grade, I devoured Richard Preston's non-fiction nightmare, *The Hot Zone*. Had I not had a terrible mind for math and chemistry, I would have gone to college to become a virologist. I watched *Outbreak* and *12 Monkeys* a hundred times. I marveled at seeing the train station at Fort Riley, Kansas, as the suspected birthplace of the 1918 "Spanish Flu" in America.

Pandemics have been a long time special interest, and the subject feels like a familiar friend. Reading books and watching documentaries gives me such a feeling of wonder and satisfaction. When I am engaging with one of my interests, the rest of the world can melt away. I am completely present and totally invested in the subject. I will skip sleep, cancel plans, and take them with me to places I must be. I've read through classes and seminars. I've worked on 2 hours of sleep. I will not let go until it lets go of me.

Go ahead, ask me about it.

Over the years, I've had many intense interests that have brought me a lot of enjoyment, including The Titanic, Great White sharks, natural disasters, true crime (including specific cases like Jack the Ripper), cats, The Legend of Sleepy Hollow, analyzing horror movies, cozy mysteries, witch hunts including the Salem Witch Trials, mental health, and Autism. All of these hold a special place in my heart, and some are long-lasting. Others I have put on a shelf. I don't control how that happens.

My husband is also likely Autistic, though it has not been officially diagnosed. He has currently been on a woodworking kick since we had some trees cut down at our old house. He's been working on making his own workbench for about three months. On the weekends, I have to go get him to eat. That's his happy place, sawing wood and watching YouTube videos in the basement.

My daughter loves everything French. We have a 6-foot-tall Eiffel Tower in our living room and four dozen books on France, French food, and French lifestyle. We visit a French bakery four or five times a week. We once watched the Olson Twins movie in Paris for six months straight.

This isn't unusual. **Autistics, as well as some other neurodivergent people, tend to deeply focus on a small number of interests at a time.** This goes by many names, including "restrictive interests," "obsessions," "fixations," "hyperfixations," "special interests," "specialized interests," "SpIns," and "monotropism." This focus is a part of the diagnostic criteria for Autism, but what matters is that it's part of the identity of Autistic people. In fact, I can't imagine a life without intense interests.

<u>Monotropism</u> is a theory introduced by Autistic researcher Dr. Dinah Murray and states that neurodivergent people, including Autistic, ADHD, and those with a mixed neurotype of two, have nervous systems that dictate deep focus in fewer subjects.[85] Monotropism is a method of not only explaining special interests but to understand Autism itself.

Monotropism as a Cognitive Style

Monotropism represents a cognitive style for Autistic and some other neurodivergent people where laser focus rules. Fergus Murray, the son of Dinah Murray, calls these "attention tunnels."[86] In this place of immersion in this one thing, Autistics achieve mindfulness and can enter a flow state, or so-called "task immersion," where a person becomes enmeshed with the task and wholly absorbed. As an Autistic person, I'm unsure how entering a flow state sounds to a non-Autistic person's ears; for me, that's the goal of goals — actualization.

Therefore, the Autistic brain's habit through wiring is to process information in such a way that it prioritizes a single, intensely focused interest or stimulus over a broad range of external inputs. This tendency to hyperfocus on

---

[85] Murray, D., Lesser, M., & Lawson, W. (2005). Attention, monotropism and the diagnostic criteria for autism. *Autism : the international journal of research and practice, 9*(2), 139–156. https://doi.org/10.1177/1362361305051398

[86] Murray, F. (2018). Me and monotropism: A unified theory of Autism. The British Psychological Society. Retrieved from https://www.bps.org.uk/psychologist/me-and-monotropism-unified-theory-autism

specific topics, activities, or sensory experiences can result in a deep engagement and thorough exploration of a particular subject, often leading to expertise or mastery in that area. **Monotropism is what makes Autistics specialists.**

The monotropic mind is drawn deeply into one interest at a time, allocating a disproportionate amount of attention and processing resources to that focal point. So, while the non-Autistic person can easily switch tasks, "hold that thought," and "circle back," the Autistic brain sees no reason to do this. While the Autistic brain is getting rewards from engaging in this interest, others like teachers, employers, or family members see resistance to shifting attention away from the current focus, difficulty in transitioning between tasks, and a predisposition towards "perseveration" or "repetitive behaviors" related to the chosen interest.

This is a result of an orientation towards acting like a neurotypical. In other words, the non-Autistics in the lives of Autistic people want them to adjust to demands and schedules and to doing things they don't want to do without recognizing that this is a design and not a defect. The design is a nervous system made for this.

The Interest-Based Nervous System

The idea of an interest-based nervous system posits that the mind operates as an "interest system," where individuals are naturally inclined towards specific interests that shape their thinking and direct their attention.

In this model, interests are not merely fleeting preferences but rather powerful forces that guide attention, perception, and behavior. Each person's interest system is unique, reflecting their individual passions, curiosities, and motivations. The intensity, salience, and permanence of these interests vary, influencing the individual's engagement with the world around them. Within the context of Autism, the interest-based nervous system underscores the central role of focused interests in shaping Autistic cognition and behavior, providing a context to understand the distinctive patterns of attention and engagement characteristic of Autistic people.

For Autistic people, "interests" aren't just interesting. They are driving forces of nature that pull us in. There is a lovely little visual for this I want to share with you from the 2001 film *Donnie Darko* starring Jake Gyllenhall. The film is worth a watch on its own merits, but there are a couple of scenes where Donnie (Gyllenhall) begins to see the ethereal manifestation of people's desires in the form of a stream of liquid energy emanating from their chests. He sees his little sister chasing the energy of her desire around the house as she runs in circles. He sees his dad's go towards the fridge for a beer. He sees his own go towards his new girlfriend.

When I saw this movie in the theater in 2001, I was struck by how accurately the visuals lined up with my experience of desires. They aren't mere ideas; my desires have tangibility, and they have to be followed and cared for. Not following those desires causes distress that I can feel physically. To further demonstrate this, I once had a friend of my husband tell me, "I wouldn't want to stand between you and something you wanted." I'm pretty sure he didn't mean it as a compliment, but my ambition and my drive haven't diminished in response to the discomfort of men.

While stimming behaviors aren't strictly interests, they are a part of the category of "restrictive and repetitive behaviors" under the medical model. Research and experience routinely support that interrupting Autistic people engaging in repetitive behaviors can lead to meltdowns.[87]

How does Monotropism Explain Autism?

Monotropism isn't only about special interests. Monotropism serves as an Autistic-defined unifying theory of Autism, meaning that monotropism can be used to explain the traits of Autism. Murray's theory offers a compelling explanation for the core features of Autism by demonstrating how attentional differences influence various aspects of Autistic thinking and behavior.

According to the theory of monotropism, as defined by Dinah Murray and discussed by Fergus Murray, the tendency towards monotropic attention:

---

[87] Leon, Y., Lazarchick, W. N., Rooker, G. W., & DeLeon, I. G. (2013). Assessment of problem behavior evoked by disruption of ritualistic toy arrangements in a child with autism. *Journal of applied behavior analysis*, 46(2), 507–511. https://doi.org/10.1002/jaba.41

1. <u>Focused interests and behavior:</u> The tendency towards specializing leads to a heightened focus on specific interests or activities, often to the exclusion of competing stimuli or tasks. This is what I refer to as specializing. Autistic brains are specialists—Subject Matter Experts. This intense focus can manifest as **Autistic inertia, wherein individuals experience difficulty initiating, transitioning, or disengaging from activities due to the overwhelming pull of their current interest.**

2. <u>Sensory Differences:</u> Additionally, monotropism accounts for sensory differences commonly observed in Autism, as individuals may struggle to process multiple sensory inputs simultaneously, leading to either hyper- or hypo-sensitivity to sensory stimuli.

3. <u>Comfort in Sameness:</u> Monotropism can also explain the drive to maintain routines. Not only are routines beneficial if you value specific things, but having the ability to go on autopilot and repeat the same routines frees up mental space to focus on your interests.

4. <u>Social Differences:</u> Social differences in Autism, such as challenges in communication and social interaction, are also attributed to monotropic processing, as individuals may prioritize their internal focus over external social cues, leading to difficulties in navigating social situations.

5. <u>Executive Functions:</u> How easy is it to make your dental appointment when you're studying the most important thing ever?

The Role of Special Interests

The most important role of special interests is their value to Autistic people. Special interests often serve as a source of comfort, joy, and self-expression for Autistics, and can even provide a means of healthy escape from overwhelming sensory experiences or social demands. They can also serve other purposes.

Special interests play a multifaceted role in society and perhaps even evolution, with implications not just for individual well-being and creativity but also for survival, adaptation, and social cohesion. These intense passions can also fuel exceptional talent and expertise in specific domains, contributing to advancements in science, technology, arts, and culture.

You've probably seen lists of famous scientists and artists with Autistic traits, like Leonardo Davinci, Isaac Newton, and Alan Turing. Albert Einstein had a speech delay and struggled with social interactions, preferring his own company. He had learning difficulties in his early education. He was a dedicated thinker with a great deal of focus. He limited his wardrobe options to reduce the need to make frivolous decisions.[88]

Emily Dickinson had epilepsy, a condition that co-occurs with Autism about 30% of the time. She wrote poetry religiously and often about topics relating to the experiences of Autistic people, like feeling separate. She had a strong affinity for nature and gardened constantly. She never married.

Each of these figures brought themselves joy and accomplishment in their focused interests, and we collectively benefited from the labor as well. Autistics bring something different to the table, and society benefits from that.

From an evolutionary perspective, the prevalence of special interests in Autistics may reflect a diversity of cognitive strategies within the human population, with monotropic minds offering unique perspectives and problem-solving approaches that enrich societal development and adaptation for humans as a species. My husband fights me on this, saying that there's no design in evolution.[89] Whether it's simply natural selection at work or some brilliance in our DNA, the result is that some minds propel us forward with

---

[88] James I. (2003). Singular scientists. *Journal of the Royal Society of Medicine, 96*(1), 36–39. https://doi.org/10.1177/014107680309600112

[89] R. Clements, (personal communication, January 23, 2024) believes that it's nonsense to attribute design to evolution, no matter how cool or intelligent it seems.

their point of view, innovation, and unique problem-solving abilities. For many, special interests can lead to careers, but **passions do not have to turn into profit**.

Further, shared enthusiasm for common interests can foster connections and community among individuals with similar passions, promoting social inclusion and a sense of belonging. Autistic people connect over their passions. Special interests can be used to forge strong bonds.

How to Ethically Use Special Interests in Teaching and Learning

Families, teachers, and therapists can ethically harness special interests to support learning and development in Autistics by recognizing and validating their significance, using them to promote connection through *genuine* interest, and refusing to withhold them as punishment or use them as a reward.

Rather than viewing special interests as distractions or obstacles to learning, educators, families, and therapists can incorporate them into curriculum planning, individualized learning strategies, and activities. By leveraging the motivational power of special interests, those who love and work with Autistic people can enhance the Autistic person's engagement, autonomy, and achievement across various domains. This can be done by engaging with the Autistic person in talk, play, joint attention, and in studying the child or adult's interests.

For example, if the Autistic person has a special interest in France, learn about France. If the individual is able, let them teach you. Then, bring France into the lesson you are teaching. Learning to tie shoes? Look at French footwear. Is there a French style of shoe tying? Use French terms.

If their interest doesn't lend itself to such practical matters, such as fans or vacuums or something else, get creative. What would happen if your loose shoelace got caught in a vacuum? By joining with the individual in their interests, you are showing them you are interested *in them*.

Many approaches to teaching use Behaviorism, which is an approach that uses conditioning, usually through rewards and punishments. Often, Autistic and other children and adults are subjected to reward systems where they earn access to the things they love. You might be saying, "Yeah, of course, that's canned motivation to use to get them to do what they don't want to do!" I suggest that you resist this urge. Autistic people are highly sensitive to manipulation, and attempting to change behavior by controlling access to interests is manipulation.

This can cause the individual to soon hate their interest because you have ruined it for them. This can cause the individual to direct those negative feelings toward you because withholding their interest to use as a reward feels like a punishment. Rewards can also feel like demands on their behaviors, which they are, and that can cause them to refuse. Finally, encouraging Autistics to do things they do not want to do to get a reward can inadvertently set them up to do other things they do not want to do through offers of rewards, punishments, or coercion. **When Autistics spend too much time uncomfortable for the benefit of others, they forget the difference between therapy or learning and abuse.**

Fostering a supportive and inclusive learning environment that celebrates diverse interests and talents encourages the exploration and expression of individual passions. Those passions should be a part of learning, and they should never be withheld. Collaborating with Autistics to identify ways their special interests can be integrated into learning experiences promotes a strengths-based approach to education or therapy that honors the unique cognitive styles and strengths of Autistic people. And even if it doesn't lead to more cooperation and acquiescence, it is the right thing to honor autonomy. **You will never win a power struggle with an Autistic person and leave them unscathed.**

Benefits of monotropism

Intense love for something is its own reward. **The benefit of monotropism is Autistic joy.** Other benefits are specialization and expertise that might be finding fulfillment in a related pastime, job, or career. Highly focused interests can lead to skill-building. Connecting to others over a shared interest is a highly valued experience for Autistic people. Monotropism is what makes Autistic people highly specialized subject matter experts.

Disadvantages of monotropism

Monotropism can also be seen as limiting. It can limit skills and limit the breadth of knowledge. This is generally an outside perspective. This singular focus can come with some stigma from neurotypical people. Related is the social cost of not always having an interest in what others are sharing. Most Autistics have multiple interests or something that changes over time, so it's simplistic to believe that Autistics are only focused on one single topic. It's more like one topic at a time.

Summary

Monotropism is both the tendency for Autistic brains to focus deeply on a narrow range of things at a time and a theory of Autism. It is intense interest and specialization in topics that shape thinking and attention patterns. While monotropism can lead to expertise and personal fulfillment, it can also present challenges when neurotypical people want Autistics to attend to other things. Special interests are celebrated in the Autistic community for fostering connections, driving innovation, and shaping individual identity, but most of all, for the joy they bring. The chapter emphasizes the importance of understanding and ethically incorporating special interests into learning and development practices to promote happiness, skill-building, and connection. The goal of special interests should not be to meet the demands of capitalism.

The takeaway for Autistics

Your special interests matter. They do so much for you. They belong to you. You don't have to earn them. They might lead you anywhere, but they don't have to pay for themselves. They don't have to pay at all. You're not required to turn joy into a paycheck.

Tips

1. **Love what you love:** Whatever it is that sparks your interest is valid and great. It doesn't have to be anything impressive or "useful." The only thing to watch out for is things that are harmful. It's ok if you love Monster High and you're 40. It's ok if you love knitting and you're a 20-year-old.

2. **New or old, both are ok:** It's ok for your interests to change. It doesn't have any greater meaning. However, if you feel you've lost all interest in anything, you may be experiencing burnout or depression. In that case, you may need extra support.

3. **Camaraderie:** Find others who love the thing, too. They are out there waiting to get happy about the latest news.

The takeaway for those who love or work with Autistics

This is how you connect to the Autistic people in your life. Validate those interests. Share in them. Special interests are an aspect of the Autistic experience that is both one of the most important and one of the most ignored by others. Just because it's not important to you doesn't make it unimportant.

Autistic thinking is driven by interest. For the Autistic child trying to tell you about Minecraft, this is the most important thing in the world. Sharing it with you is a sign of love and affection. For the Autistic adult telling you about the moon rover or the 1968 protests at the Democratic Convention, the intricacies of the Real Housewives, or training their dog: this is relating. This is friendship. This is love. Support them by listening, commenting, and asking questions when appropriate. It's never to be used to manipulate behavior. It's for joy and connection. That's more than enough.

Tips

1. **Remember who the Experts are:** Treat Autistic people as experts in their interests (and experts in themselves).

2. **Learn about their interest:** This is important. When you wing it, you will be discovered!

3. **Engage in Their Interests:** Bring their interests into your interactions. Do not use it as a reward or a punishment.

4. **A Little Variety:** Remember that Autistics may have more than one interest, and their interests may change. Adapt with them.

Chapter 5
Executive Functioning: Adulting and Other Misadventures

Executive functions are like the personal assistants of the brain, tasked with keeping everything running smoothly in the chaotic office of life. They are your calendar, filing system, office persona, your vision board, your five-year plan. I am both Autistic and ADHD. I have two assistants who both work part-time. Sometimes, my personal assistant is Alfred Pennyworth or Pepper Potts, who has everything under control, thinks of all the details, and plans for them in meticulous detail. Other times, my personal assistant is like Drop Dead Fred, Beetlejuice, or Jack Sparrow. They enjoy chaos on its own merits and reject your system just because.

Executive functions (EF) are a set of cognitive and emotional processes that encompass a range of higher-order mental abilities involved in goal-directed behavior, problem-solving, self-regulation, and adaptive decision-making.[90] In other words, executive functions are the brain's tools for helping us plan, solve problems, control our

---

[90] Cristofori, I., Cohen-Zimerman, S., & Grafman, J. (2019). Executive functions. *Handbook of clinical neurology, 163*, 197–219. https://doi.org/10.1016/B978-0-12-804281-6.00011-2

impulses, and make good choices. The EF are the adults of the brain. They can be thought of as cognitive skills that control other cognitive and emotional skills. In this chapter, we will discuss the role of executive functions in Autistic thinking and everyday life.

The Role of Executive Functions in Daily Life

From the moment we wake up to the time we go to bed, executive functions shape how we navigate tasks, solve problems, and regulate our behavior. Imagine trying to juggle multiple responsibilities without the ability to plan ahead or shift focus when needed—if you're neurodivergent, you probably don't have to imagine. If you're neurotypical, you might think these abilities are innate and learning them is just a part of becoming an adult, but my friend, surprise! It's not something you've honed with the sheer power of your mighty will; it's just the way your brain works.[91] Most brains have the systems in place to be able to adhere to typical notions of adulthood.

Whether it's managing our time, organizing our thoughts, or resisting distractions, executive functions are the "behind-the-scenes heroes" that keep our daily lives humming along smoothly—or doing a Tokyo drift into the unknown, whatever the case may be.

---

[91] Sapolsky, R. (2023). *Determined: A science of life without free will.* Penguin Press.

Think about the last time you had to make a tough decision or resist the temptation to procrastinate or plan a semester of classes around your job and personal responsibilities—those are executive functions in action. These are the mental tools we use to weigh the pros and cons, anticipate consequences, and stay on track toward our goals. At work, school, or navigating social situations, executive functions are what help us adapt to changing circumstances and make choices that align with our values and priorities. In essence, they're the adultier adults of the brain. And for those with neurodivergent neurotypes, our brains do not function or prioritize the same way as neurotypical brains. You're more likely to hear the term "executive dysfunction" associated with Autism or ADHD. Here, we are going to acknowledge that not having the same priorities or ability to remember and enact upon those priorities is a disability, but also, *there's beauty in chaos* and the ability to make some improvements over time.

Executive Functions and the Neurodiversity Paradigm

Autistic people possess unique modes of processing that shape their cognitive strengths and differences and way of engaging with the world. Executive functions, serving as the cognitive orchestrators of thought and behavior, play a pivotal role in shaping these distinctive patterns of thinking.

Neurotypical approaches view deviations from typical executive functions as problems to be fixed — the "failure to launch," "lazy," and "never wants to grow up" narrative. The neurodiversity paradigm embraces and honors the unique ways neurodivergent individuals process information and show up in the world. This view offers support where needed and acceptance of all differences with an assumption of good intentions. **Within the neurodiversity paradigm, executive functions are not viewed solely through a deficit lens but rather as part of a different way of being that has benefits as well as drawbacks.**

At the heart of the neurodiversity paradigm is a fundamental respect for the autonomy and agency of Autistics and other neurodivergent people as valuable in their own right. By reframing executive functions within this paradigm, we shift away from a deficit model, where Autistics must change to operate in the "real world," toward a more holistic understanding of cognitive variation. This paradigm acknowledges that while aspects of executive functioning may present challenges or even sometimes insurmountable obstacles without accommodation, they also allow for the use of strengths and alternative ways of problem-solving and understanding the world.

Embracing neurodiversity and the diversity within the Autistic neurotype — including those parts that are disabling — fosters acceptance, empowerment, and inclusion, and an expectation of accommodating others where individuals are valued for their distinctive perspectives and contributions but are also just accepted as they are.

I'm not a huge fan of stereotypes, but there's one in this realm that I do like: the absent-minded professor. This trope is pretty well known. The absent-minder professor is an academic with a high degree of specialty in their subject, and basically, everything else falls by the wayside. The 1961 film of the same title is the classic movie about the professor who invents a substance that increases its stored energy each time it strikes a surface—flubber.[92] It was also remade in 1997 under the name *Flubber*, starring Robin Williams.[93] In both films, the professor even misses his own wedding due to his focus on his scientific pursuits. What I love about this trope is that people tend to accept the character as they are even though they get fed up with some of the EF the character displays. The characters don't change, either. They do eventually meet their obligations. Before I knew about Autism, this is how I referred to my husband. Sadly, most of these characters are white men.

The Home of the Executive Functions in the Brain

The home of the executive functions (EF) is the prefrontal cortex (PFC), which is, for the most part, the area of your brain behind your forehead. It's the part of the brain that

---

* [92] Stevenson, R. (1961). *The Absent Minded Professor* [Film]. Walt Disney Studios Motion Pictures.

* [93] Mayfield, L. (1997). *Flubber* [Film]. Walt Disney Pictures.

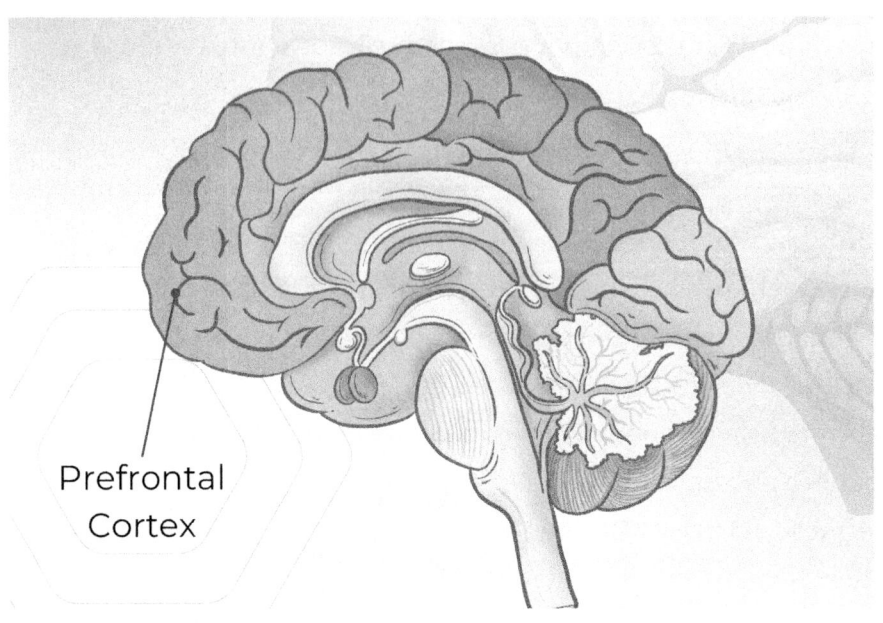

Prefrontal Cortex

matures last, which is why we tend to think of EF as signs of maturity. However, it's really a function of neural connections rather than will.

Components of Executive Functions

Depending on how you categorize them, there can be a dozen or more executive functions. Many of these operate differently in Autistic people as well as those with other neurodivergences, sometimes spectacularly different. But as with everything in Autism, the executive functions manifest differently from Autistic person to Autistic person. As we explore executive functions, we will review how these *may* show up in Autistic people. **Please note that while some EF** are routinely found to be difficult for Autistic people, some research and experience show that others are areas where at least some Autistic people excel, such as problem-solving, planning, and verbal fluency.[94] Technology and other assistive methods are shown to improve areas when support is needed.[95] Something to remember about EF is that Autistic people will learn and make adjustments over time based on their ability to do so, which varies from person to person.

Hot and Cold Executive Functions

Hot and cold EF is a way to categorize them into those that are related to emotions — hot — and those that are related to cognition only — cold.[96]

Hot EF

1. **Emotional regulation:** Emotional regulation involves understanding our own emotional cues and controlling the intensity of our emotions and our related behaviors.

---

[94] St. John, T., Woods, S., Bode, T., Ritter, C., & Estes, A. (2022). A review of executive functioning challenges and strengths in autistic adults. *The Clinical Neuropsychologist*, 36(5), 1116-1147. https://doi.org/10.1080/13854046.2021.1971767

[95] Desideri, L., Di Santantonio, A., Varrucciu, N., Bonsi, I., & Di Sarro, R. (2020). Assistive technology for cognition to support executive functions in autism: A scoping review. *Advances in Neurodevelopmental Disorders*, 4(4), 330-343. https://doi.org/10.1007/s41252-020-00163-w

[96] Salehinejad, M. A., Ghanavati, E., Rashid, M. H. A., & Nitsche, M. A. (2021). Hot and cold executive functions in the brain: A prefrontal-cingular network. *Brain and Neuroscience Advances*, 5. https://doi.org/10.1177/23982128211007769

Emotional regulation includes attention, such as moving our attention away from the thing that is activating us, trying to think about the issue differently, and modulating the way we express our emotions.[97] Autistics are known to have different emotional responses, sometimes bigger, sometimes smaller, and sometimes delayed. Autistics may also have difficulty controlling their expression of emotions.[98] The emotional experience of Autistics isn't uniform, and what is seen from the outside may not reflect what is happening inside.

2. **Impulse control and inhibition:** Many of the executive functions are about proactively getting things done, but this one is about controlling one's self, including creating a gap between a stimulus and a reaction to consider that reaction, controlling impulses to engage in problematic behaviors like self-harm, acting out towards another person, shopping, eating, or using substances, and resisting distractions. Autistic people are known to have difficulty in all of these areas. Autistics are twice as likely to use alcohol

---

[97] Wadlinger, H. A., & Isaacowitz, D. M. (2011). Fixing our focus: training attention to regulate emotion. Personality and social psychology review: an official journal of the Society for Personality and Social Psychology, Inc, 15(1), 75–102. https://doi.org/10.1177/1088868310365565

[98] Mazefsky, C. A., Herrington, J., Siegel, M., Scarpa, A., Maddox, B. B., Scahill, L., & White, S. W. (2013). The role of emotion regulation in autism spectrum disorder. *Journal of the American Academy of Child and Adolescent Psychiatry, 52*(7), 679–688. https://doi.org/10.1016/j.jaac.2013.05.006

or drugs to a harmful degree.[99] Parents report that 68% of Autistic children and adolescents have acted out physically on them at least once.[100] At least 24% of Autistics report or are observed to engage in self-harming behaviors.[101]

3. **Self-Monitoring:** This executive function involves the ability to evaluate one's own behavior, performance, and progress toward goals, as well as to adjust behaviors or strategies accordingly and in real time. Autistics may experience challenges with self-monitoring due to difficulties in recognizing social cues, understanding social norms, and processing feedback, including interoception in childhood and beyond.[102] These difficulties can impact various aspects of life, including academic performance, social relationships, and self-care routines. The development of self-monitoring skills in Autistics can enhance the ability to self-regulate, make informed decisions, and advocate for their needs.

---

[99] Butwicka, A., Långström, N., Larsson, H., Lundström, S., Serlachius, E., Almqvist, C., Frisén, L., & Lichtenstein, P. (2017). Increased Risk for Substance Use-Related Problems in Autism Spectrum Disorders: A Population-Based Cohort Study. *Journal of autism and developmental disorders, 47*(1), 80–89. https://doi.org/10.1007/s10803-016-2914-2

[100] Kanne, S. M., & Mazurek, M. O. (2011). Aggression in children and adolescents with ASD: prevalence and risk factors. *Journal of autism and developmental disorders, 41*(7), 926–937. https://doi.org/10.1007/s10803-010-1118-4

[101] Licence, L., Oliver, C., Moss, J. et al. (2020). Prevalence and Risk-Markers of Self-Harm in Autistic Children and Adults. *Journal of Autism and Developmental Disorders* **50**, 3561–3574. https://doi.org/10.1007/s10803-019-04260-1

[102] Fong, V. C., & Iarocci, G. (2020). The role of executive functioning in predicting social competence in children with and without autism spectrum disorder. *Autism Research, 13*(11), 1856-1866. https://doi.org/10.1002/aur.2350

Cold EF

4. **Cognitive flexibility:** This is a person's ability to switch between two types of thinking in order to respond quickly and appropriately.[103] It can be thought of as "mental agility." This involves switching attention and moving between different sets of rules and tasks. Examples include debating, multitasking, and working on two different projects at once. Autistic people tend to have more difficulty with cognitive flexibility, which makes sense when you consider the strengths of Autistics lie in focusing exclusively on one thing at a time. Practice can improve flexibility, but accomodations are needed for most.

5. **Working Memory**: Working memory is the capacity to hold and manipulate information in mind over short periods to complete tasks, such as remembering someone's name they just told you, directions or instructions you were just given, or remembering a phone number just told to you. Autistic people are more likely to have a hard time with specific types of working memory.[104] These differences can have a direct impact on relationships with others, especially when authorities fail to understand these

---

[103] Dajani, D. R., & Uddin, L. Q. (2015). Demystifying cognitive flexibility: Implications for clinical and developmental neuroscience. *Trends in neurosciences*, 38(9), 571–578. https://doi.org/10.1016/j.tins.2015.07.003

[104] Kercood, S., Grskovic, J. A., Banda, D., & Begeske, J. (2014). Working memory and autism: A review of literature. *Research in autism spectrum disorders*, 8(10), 1316-1332. https://doi.org/10.1016/j.rasd.2014.06.011

differences. If teachers and parents believe that something just told to a child will be remembered, then they may assign willful disobedience to what is actually a part of their normal Autistic processing.

6. **Planning, Organization, and Goal-setting:** This executive function encompasses the ability to set goals, develop strategies, and arrange tasks or activities in a logical sequence to achieve desired outcomes. Autistics may struggle with planning and organization due to challenges in cognitive flexibility, sensory processing differences, and difficulty with self-initiation, but this can also be explained by monotropism.[105] When a person's goal is to be waist-deep in the topic, looking at a dozen variables and plotting them on a calendar is daunting and disinteresting. Difficulties with planning and organization can manifest in various aspects of life, including academic performance, time management, and independent living skills.[106] The development of planning and organization skills in Autistics can enhance their ability to navigate daily tasks and promote greater confidence and autonomy. This can take some creativity and effort to find an individual approach that works.

---

[105] Murray, F. (2018). Me and monotropism: A unified theory of Autism. The British Psychological Society. Retrieved from https://www.bps.org.uk/psychologist/me-and-monotropism-unified-theory-autism

[106] Hill, E. L. (2004). Evaluating the theory of executive dysfunction in autism. *Developmental review*, 24(2), 189-233. https://doi.org/10.1016/j.dr.2004.01.001

7. **Reasoning, Decision-making, and Problem-solving:** Problem-solving is the aptitude to identify, analyze, and generate solutions to complex or novel problems. Autistics may struggle with problem-solving due to difficulties in cognitive flexibility, abstract reasoning, anxiety, and understanding social cues, while others may excel at problem-solving due to focused attention to detail and lateral thinking. Difficulties in problem-solving can impact various areas of life, including navigating social situations, completing academic assignments, and adapting to new environments. However, innovative problem-solving by Autistics can also sometimes be rejected by neurotypical people. The development of problem-solving skills in Autistics is helpful for fostering independence and promoting successful outcomes across different domains.[107] But Autistics think differently, and neurotypical methods may not be useful.

8. **Initiation:** Initiation as an EF is about getting started and staying the course to completion. It's the cognitive process that involves the capacity to independently begin tasks or activities and sustain the effort of completing them. Autistics may encounter challenges with initiation due to difficulties in task-switching, transitioning between activities, and regulating attention. Autistic inertia is a term used to describe issues with task initiation and task-

---

[107] Merchan-Naranjo, J., Boada, L., del Rey-Mejias, A., Mayoral, M., Llorente, C., Arango, C., & Parellada, M. (2016). Executive function is affected in autism spectrum disorder, but does not correlate with intelligence. *Revista de Psiquiatría y Salud Mental (English Edition)*, 9(1), 39-50. https://doi.org/10.1016/j.rpsmen.2016.01.001

switching. These challenges can manifest in various settings, such as academic settings, employment, and daily routines. The development of initiation skills in Autistic people can support goal attainment, but accommodations may continue to be needed.

9. **Time Management:** Time management first requires time-awareness. Autistic people may experience time differently. Some Autistic people rely on time to serve as a trigger for actions, while others might be more in the "time's not real" camp. Time Management involves the ability to allocate time efficiently, understand how long tasks may take, prioritize tasks, and meet deadlines. Autistics may face challenges with time management due to difficulties in estimating time, organizing tasks, and shifting focus between activities, and time not, you know, being real. These challenges can impact various aspects of life, including academic performance, employment, and daily routines. The development of time management skills in Autistics can, most importantly, reduce stress when operating in a neurotypical world. For those who struggle with this, technology is a good form of accommodation.

Concrete, Abstract, and Critical Thinking

Concrete thinking is defined as reasoning that you tangibly experience through the senses.[108] It's also known as literal thinking. Autistics often exhibit strong concrete thinking skills, which enable them to focus on details and process information in a precise and logical manner. This cognitive strength can lead to exceptional abilities in problem-solving, pattern recognition, and analytical thinking.

An example of concrete thinking from my own life is that I only know when people are "joking" by telling me something that is factually incorrect about half the time. I take what people say at face value. My experience in the world is that people are unpredictable, and anything is possible, so when my friend jokingly tells me she left her husband, I believe it because he's kind of a jerk anyway. (Autistic people also have a sense of humor, see?)

Concrete thinking may not be the whole story for Autistic people. A better way to think of this in total is that Autistics use knowledge and understanding they have experienced. By embracing their natural inclination towards

---

* [108] APA Dictionary of Psychology, concrete thinking. (2024). American Psychological Association. https://dictionary.apa.org/concrete-thinking

concrete thinking, Autistics can excel in tasks that require attention to detail and sequential processing. However, with exposure to more information and the opportunity to explore it, Autistics may be able to access and utilize more abstract thinking as well.

Abstract thinking is defined as thinking in generalized concepts and ideas that aren't immediate or tangible,[109] **which can involve processing complex social cues, nuances, and ambiguities, which can be more challenging for some Autistics. Examples of abstract thinking include emotions like love and concepts like metaphors.**

I can learn abstract concepts, but there are some that I can't make sense of. I understand love deeply, as many Autistic people do, but the desire to climb a mountain "because it's there" does not compute.

By acknowledging and accepting this difference, we can work to create supportive environments that accommodate Autistic thinking styles. This might include providing explicit instructions, using visual aids to facilitate understanding, and encouraging Autistics to ask questions and seek clarification without social punishment for doing so.

---

* [109] APA Dictionary of Psychology, abstract thinking. (2024). American Psychological Association. https://dictionary.apa.org/abstract-thinking

Critical Thinking

Critical thinking is an analytical assessment of a subject that resists intuitive suppositions and is independent in its approach. It allows for nuance and grey areas. Some parts of critical thinking are tailor-made for Autistics, while some require support and time to process.

Autistics often exhibit these skills that align with critical thinking:

1. **Attention to detail:** Autistics tend to be detail-oriented, which helps them analyze information thoroughly.

2. **Logical reasoning:** Autistics often think in a logical and systematic way, allowing them to evaluate information objectively.

3. **Analysis:** Autistics tend to break down complex information into smaller parts, analyzing each component carefully.

4. **Independence of thought:** Autistics are often less influenced by social norms and biases, allowing them to think more independently and critically.[110]

---

* [110] Morsanyi, K., & Hamilton, J. (2023). The Development of Intuitive and Analytic Thinking in Autism: The Case of Cognitive Reflection. *Journal of Intelligence*, 11(6), 124. https://doi.org/10.3390/jintelligence11060124

These are skills that vary widely within the community. Not all Autistics will exhibit these traits to the same degree. Additionally, Autistics may need accommodations or support to fully express their critical thinking abilities.

Executive Functions and "Adulting"

Maturity and Autism are complex topics. Research shows that Autistic children lag behind their peers in social development.[111] However, it's also common for them to be drawn to adults instead of children and show advanced interests and vocabulary, and enjoy talking about those subjects. Similarly, Autistic adults may not conform to traditional expectations of adulthood, often retaining deeply loved childhood interests that others might view as immature. **In this conversation, remember that all of these assumptions about what is mature and appropriate are socially constructed, not absolute truths.**

Autistic people may seem less mature for their age for other reasons as well. Autistic adults tend to be interest-driven and not socially driven, making them less likely to hide interests that might be seen as age-inappropriate. Autistics tend to have different experiences and expressions of emotion,

---

[111] Maddox, B. B., Cleary, P., Kuschner, E. S., Miller, J. S., Armour, A. C., Guy, L., Kenworthy, L., Schultz, R. T., & Yerys, B. E. (2018). Lagging skills contribute to challenging behaviors in children with autism spectrum disorder without intellectual disability. *Autism : the international journal of research and practice*, 22(8), 898–906. https://doi.org/10.1177/1362361317712651

which may be less controlled than in neurotypical people. Finally, having trouble with executive functioning tasks when compared to typical peers, Autistic people again seem less mature in the estimation of neurotypical people who do not have the same struggles. Executive functions are the adults of the brain, and for many Autistics, carrying out some of these tasks feels like an imitation of adulthood. It can feel unnatural.

Adulting as an Autistic person may conflict and interfere with our interests, competing for our precious time. When the skills to "adult" aren't natural for us, we may struggle with work, relationships, and everyday living tasks. However, we can also adapt our lifestyles in numerous ways that support our brains when we can control the environment.

At Work

In the workplace, Autistics may encounter difficulties with time management, task prioritization, and social interactions, impacting their performance and job satisfaction. Challenges in initiating tasks, maintaining focus, and managing sensory sensitivities can also affect their ability to meet job expectations and adapt to workplace environments.

Many Autistics look for jobs that are well-suited for their needs and interests, but many more struggle to work in typical 9-5 office or retail settings. The rates of unemployment are staggering. Non-traditional jobs, such as consultant and book writer (wink, wink), may be better fits for Autistic people.

At Home

In the realm of so-called independent living (people's independence is not as independent as we pretend), Autistics may have challenges in planning and organizing daily tasks, managing household responsibilities, and maintaining routines. Difficulties with executive functions such as planning, organization, impulse control, and problem-solving can impact the ability to manage finances, maintain a healthy lifestyle, and access necessary support services. Additionally, navigating transitions and changes in living situations can be particularly challenging, requiring flexibility, adaptability, and resilience.

With appropriate support and accommodations tailored to their individual needs, Autistics can develop strategies to enhance their executive functioning skills and successfully navigate the responsibilities of work and independent living.

In adulthood, implementing strategies to support executive function skills can significantly enhance the daily functioning and overall well-being of individuals, including Autistics. We'll discuss some methods for increasing successful supports in the "tips" section, but first, enjoy these tales from the EF Crypt.

Misadventures

Many of my experiences can serve as "LFMF" or learn from my fail. Here are some stories of adulting gone wrong in my life. Here's a collection of times when my executive function didn't.

Pro-tip: Ask to reschedule before your appointment to avoid a missed appointment fee

I miss about 1/4 of my own appointments. Never my daughter's appointments, and never appointments with my own clients. I always think I will remember when my appointment is, where it is, and what it's for. Unless it's something important, I have no idea. I rely on text reminders for appointments. I still end up doing Zoom appointments from my car with the audio only, showing up at the wrong office or a completely different clinic. I am always late. What is time, really? Anyway, did you know if you call just before your missed appointment and say that you need to reschedule, they usually won't charge you for missing the appointment?

I bought a fake fox

You call it impulsive. I call it spontaneous. I want to do cool things! I want to buy cool things! When the opportunity arises, I seize it. This has led to some great adventures and some funny stories. I am also the owner of a 6-foot-tall Eiffel Tower, a taxidermy bat, and a life-sized fake fox. Call it sensory enrichment.

Saying no to fun things that don't hurt seems Puritanical to me. I don't even think of my impulsivity as a shortcoming or something to quell. Not everyone agrees with me, but then, it's not their life.

That one time I really put my foot in it (as opposed to the other times)

This one is a proper story. Picture it: it's a banquet with several hundred people and a boatload of speeches on deck. I'm seated with the friend I came with and random dinner companions. One of whom is a young man in his late 20s wearing a suit. He's friendly and funny, and our table jokes and laughs as we eat before speeches resume. He is a speaker, he says.

I notice throughout the dinner that he removes a small wooden box from his pocket periodically and worries it with his thumb before returning it. It's maybe three inches by two inches and has a brass sun inlaid into the wood.

As his speech gets closer, he pulls it from his pocket more often. In between speeches, I say to my suited friend with the box, "What's that, your stash box?"

A beat passes, two, and then he says, "Actually, it's my father." He's then introduced and makes a touching speech in which he cries, reenacting a conversation he had with his father on his deathbed, and produces the box at the end.

Hey, hello there, self-monitoring and inhibitory control. Wish you'd come in earlier.

My husband installs a cat door, a bonus story

My husband is always willing to work on home projects, and we needed a cat door installed. One of our cats wants to be in our bedroom and needs to get out for eating and litter box visits. However, all doors must remain closed by order of the management (our daughter). So, he took one of the doors off the hinges and took it outside, put it on some sawhorses, and started working on it. He knows I'm particular about things being centered, so he measured and drew lines to make sure it was perfectly aligned for me.

He'd just finished cutting the opening and hadn't yet put the cat door in when I came outside and said, "Hmm, is that…the top of the door?"

That, my friends, is cognitive flexibility and, specifically, the ability to direct attention. His attention was on getting the details right. He didn't spend any time thinking about something so obvious as the correct end of the door, which does have a correct end. So, now we have a cat door and a bird door in the event we get a free-roaming feathered friend.

Executive function issues can be really challenging. There are ways to learn new skills, but not everyone is going to be able to overcome all of them with apps and good intentions. For example, I don't think I will ever master emotional regulation. Just not express emotion? Sounds fake.

Benefits of Autistic Executive Functioning

Autistic EF can result in innovation, unique approaches to problem-solving, and creativity. It's not all bad.

Disadvantages of Autistic Executive Functioning

There are also plenty of real difficulties that can arise from EF issues that can be barriers when Autistics fail to meet neurotypical expectations. These are very real and can lead to various consequences that may be minor or extreme.

Summary

Executive functions (EF) are the adults of the brain that control other cognitive functions that we associate with maturity, like controlling behaviors, time management, and planning. These functions aren't a matter of will. They are a matter of brain connectivity and function. Autistic people can and do learn some EF. They may even excel at some, but most Autistic will struggle with some EF and need self-accommodation and other supports.

Takeaway for Autistics

Executive function issues are a part of being Autistic. You likely already have put some systems in place for yourself to aid you. There will be times when something goes wrong because of your EF issues. Please take an "oops, I did it again" approach, repair what you can, and move on. You are made for important things, and you are still worthy of those things even if you are chronically late for them, overshare, or forget they exist for a while.

Strategies

Here's the part where the well-meaning author tells you to get a planner and set timers on your phone. Those are great ideas, and I do them. Writing a list every day is how I make it, but wait. That's not where we are going with this: first, you need these things before techniques:

1. **Manage expectations:** Autism is a disability. Some of us can fake some of the things, some of the time, but that takes a toll all of the time. Burnout is real, and it's always a looming threat. Autistics aren't failed neurotypicals. We aren't designed to do the same things. Managing expectations means coming to a task or event with this knowledge at the ready. Autistics themselves and others around them have to alter expectations from what a neurotypical person's expectations are.

2. **Acceptance and self-advocacy:** "So it goes" -Kurt Vonnegut
It's ok for Autistic people to be who they are. There's A LOT of hand-wringing by parents and therapists about how Autistics are going to manage in the real world. The truth is they will do things on their own if they can, and if they can't, they need support. Accepting things as they are right now doesn't mean not trying to learn new skills. It means that the Autistic person is a good, worthy person no matter what they can't do.

An Autistic person admitting when they can't do something is advocacy. Asking for support is advocacy.

3. Now, here are some things that might help. Try different techniques and see what works for you **without the expectation it will or the belief that failing is your fault.**

Mindful Planning and Flexibility
Practice mindful planning by breaking tasks into smaller, more manageable steps. Use visual aids like color-coded calendars or digital reminders to help with organization and time management. However, remain flexible and adaptable in your approach, recognizing that plans may need adjustments along the way. This takes effort upfront and pays off afterward. If this isn't the way for you, that's ok.

Sensory-Friendly Environments
Create sensory-friendly environments that minimize distractions and sensory overload. Experiment with noise-canceling headphones, fidget toys, or designated quiet spaces

to enhance focus and concentration. Conversely, you may need some stimulation to get work done instead of quiet, like a playlist or a comfort show in the background.

Self-Advocacy and Accommodations
Advocate for accommodations and support systems that cater to your individual needs. If you feel safe to do so, communicate with educators, employers, or healthcare providers about strategies or adjustments that can facilitate task completion and productivity. If they won't, try HR or social workers to help. *This type of accommodation will likely require a professional diagnosis.*

Routine and Structure
Establish consistent routines and structured schedules to provide predictability and stability *if those work well for you.* Given the rates of overlap with ADHD, this may not always be a good fit — *that's ok!* Incorporate regular breaks and downtime to prevent burnout and recharge cognitive resources. That one isn't negotiable.

Mindfulness and Stress Management
Practice mindfulness techniques, deep breathing exercises, or relaxation strategies to manage stress and regulate emotions. Cultivate self-awareness and emotional resilience to navigate challenges effectively.

Trial and Error

Experiment with various techniques and strategies to discover what works best for you. No guilt when things don't work. All discoveries are good discoveries—setbacks are opportunities for learning and growth, not personal shortcomings, even if your boss doesn't think so at the time.

By managing expectations, building self-acceptance, and exploring personalized strategies for support and accommodation, Autistics can enhance their executive function skills and navigate daily tasks with confidence and resilience. Don't forget: neurotypicality isn't the bar set for Autistic and other neurodivergent people.

Tips

1. **Acceptance:** Accept that executive function challenges are a part of this life. You're not a failure if you mess up. You're not a failure if you fail. You are a flawed character, and we are the most interesting characters.

2. **Do What Works:** You have already tried a ton of things to address these issues. Keep using the ones that work. You know yourself better than I do. I trust that you know where you need help.

3. **Support:** It's okay to ask others to pick up some tasks. You don't have to just figure it all out alone. Remember that Batman had Alfred. You can't afford an Alfred, but it's okay

to ask your partner to pay the bills or have your mom schedule your appointment.

4. **Buy a Planner:** *Just kidding.* If that hasn't worked for you, a planner won't magically fix things. If it sometimes works, try keeping it right where you work the most. And don't put a pile on top of it. Ask me how I know.

Takeaway for those who love or work with Autistics

Expect occasional (or frequent) issues with executive functioning from your Autistic loved one or client. You can support them by asking them how they think they would be best helped. However, don't be surprised if they aren't sure right away. Some methods of coping with EF issues actually require much more EF, like constantly remembering to write things on a schedule and check it. These struggles are normal for Autistic people, and they are not measures of intelligence or values. They are simply a product of brain wiring.

Tips

1. **Acceptance:** Never forget that EF issues are the result of brain wiring and not laziness or willfulness. They aren't even about maturity, either.

2. **Remove barriers:** Autistic people—like all people—will do well if they can. If you see a pattern of a specific EF issue and

think you have the exact solution, remember that this is a bright person whose brain is better at different things than this. Go ahead and talk about your idea, but be prepared to remove barriers to aid them. The goal isn't "independence." We are all much less independent than we pretend to be. The goal is to live and love.

3. **Anticipate:** Some EF issues you might see a ways off. For example, the only way I get to appointments is when I get text reminders they are happening that day. Anticipate issues and implement strategies to help.

Chapter 6
Autism and Memory: Wait, What Were We Talking About?

My earliest memory is of waking from a dream. I was asleep in my crib when I heard a strange sound, which I now recognize as the sound of an ambulance. Then, I heard running footsteps on the roof of my house, and then I looked out the window to see Spiderman crawling down the side of my house. He paused to look at me. I climbed out of my crib and ran to my mom, who was making a sandwich in the kitchen. I started speaking to her, but I didn't speak enough English yet for her to understand.

I once told my psychiatrist this story, and he listened politely and then told me it was impossible for me to actually remember this event. He said it was telling about my relationship with my mother, and actually, it was demonstrative of that, but he was still wrong. **Infantile amnesia is the apparent human-wide phenomenon in which** babies rapidly forget everything; however, this is another example of how Autistic brains differ because some Autistics do retain some very early memories.[112]

Memory is our brain's cataloging system of events, including encoding, storing, and retrieving information. It's a tool we use constantly. It plays a key role in virtually every aspect of our daily lives, shaping our experiences, decision-making, and interactions with the world. Memory enables us to learn from past experiences, anticipate future events, and navigate complex environments. It also serves as the foundation for higher-order cognitive processes like problem-solving and creativity. It's the mental framework that helps us make sense of our past, understand our present, and plan for the future.

There's a long history of study of Autism and memory, but like much of the study of Autism, theories developed from early research reached odd conclusions. In the 1960s and 70s, researchers suspected that Autism was a type of childhood amnesia as evidenced by regressions of speech and skills as well as working memory issues.[113] This is after decades of believing it was a type of childhood schizophrenia. The reality of memory for Autistic people is complex and variable.

---

[112] Power, S. D., Stewart, E., Zielke, L. G., Byrne, E. P., Douglas, A., Ortega-de San Luis, C., ... & Ryan, T. J. (2023). Immune activation state modulates infant engram expression across development. *Science Advances*, 9(45). https://doi.org/10.1126/sciadv.adg99

[113] DeLong, G. R. (1978). A neuropsychologic interpretation of infantile autism. In *Autism: A reappraisal of concepts and treatment* (pp. 207-218). Boston, MA: Springer US.

Memory in Autistic people is, like everything else, a heterogeneous mix of experiences that differ from neurotypical people and can differ from other Autistic people. There are patterns that stand out from research and experience. Broadly, memory is different for Autistic people with weaknesses and strengths compared to neurotypicals. In this chapter, we will look at how memory works and what it can look like for Autistics.

What is Memory, and How Does it Work?[114]

Before we go further, let's look at an outline of memory in humans as we know it. People have three basic systems of memory: sensory memory, short-term memory, and long-term memory. Feel free to just do **TL: DR (too long: didn't read) version:**

Memory is a complex process involving the encoding, storage, and retrieval of information, with different types of memory (sensory, short term, and long-term) having distinct characteristics and brain regions involved. Encoding converts sensory input into a storable form, storage retains the information across various brain regions, and retrieval accesses and brings the information back into conscious awareness. The entire process is influenced by various factors, including context, emotions, and priming, and involves

---

[114] Note: this entire section references: Zlotnik, G., & Vansintjan, A. (2019). Memory: An Extended Definition. *Frontiers in psychology*, 10, 2523. https://doi.org/10.3389/fpsyg.2019.02523

dynamic interactions between brain regions, chemical reactions, and cognitive processes.

Sensory memory: This type of memory holds onto sensory information from the environment for a brief duration, a maximum of just a few seconds. It holds onto sensory information for processing, including visual and auditory information.

Short-term memory (STM): This is another name for the executive function, usually called "working memory." This type of memory temporarily holds and manipulates information needed for ongoing cognitive tasks. STM has limited capacity and duration, typically lasting for a few seconds to a minute.

Long-term memory (LTM): Long-term memory stores information over extended periods, ranging from minutes to a lifetime. It can be further divided into several subtypes:

- **Declarative memory:** Involves conscious recollection of facts and events and can be further divided into:

    - **Episodic memory:** The recollection of specific events, experiences, and contextual details from one's personal past.

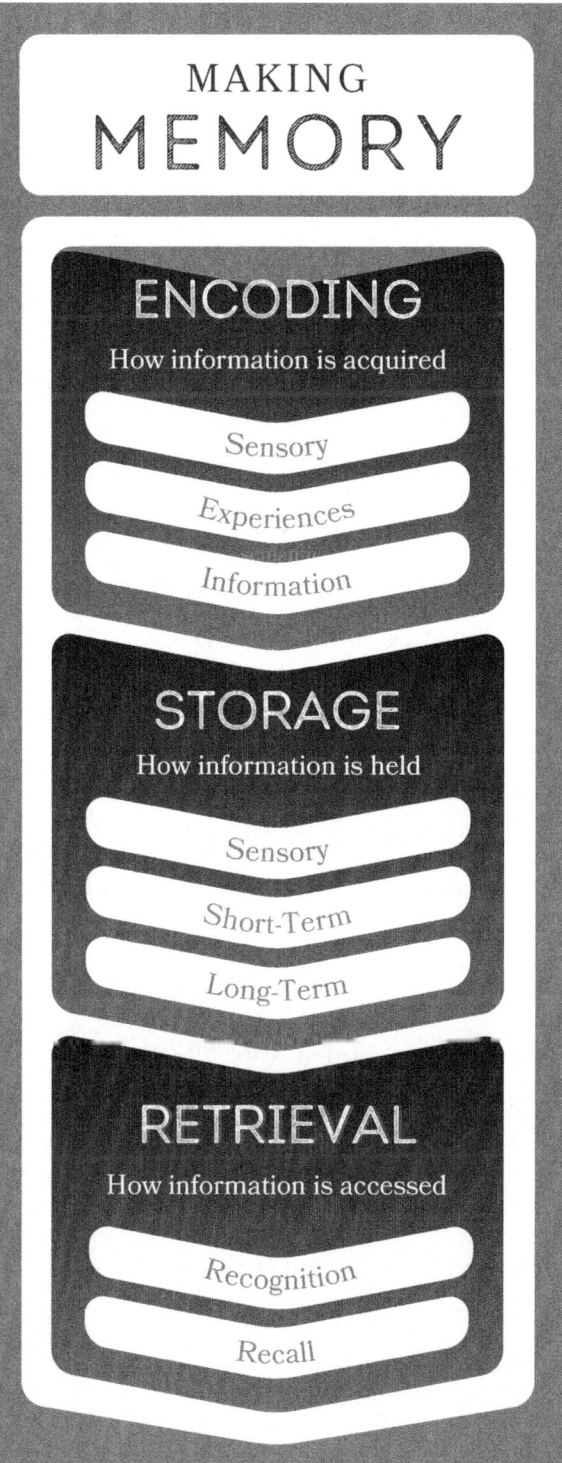

- **Semantic memory:** The retention of general knowledge, concepts, and factual information not tied to specific events.

- **Non-declarative memory:** Involves unconscious memory processes that influence behavior without conscious awareness, including:

- **Procedural memory:** Memory for skills, procedures, and how-to knowledge, such as riding a bike or tying shoelaces.

- **Priming:** Enhanced perception or identification of stimuli due to prior exposure or experience.

- **Classical conditioning:** Associative learning process in which a neutral stimulus becomes associated with a reflexive response.

Memory involves a complex process of encoding, storing, and retrieving information within the brain. Here's a discussion of each stage:

1. **Encoding:** Encoding refers to the initial process of converting sensory input into a form that can be stored in memory. Different types of encoding mechanisms are involved depending on the type of memory being formed. For example:

    - **Sensory memory:** Sensory information is encoded through sensory receptors in the corresponding sensory regions of the brain, such as visual or acoustic.

    - **Short-term memory:** Encoding in short-term memory involves the transfer of information from sensory memory to temporary storage in the prefrontal cortex and other brain regions, often through rehearsal or attentional processes.

    - **Long-term memory:** Encoding in long-term memory involves more elaborate processing, with information being transferred to regions such as the hippocampus for consolidation and integration into existing memory networks.

2. **Storage:** Once information is encoded, it needs to be stored in memory for later retrieval. Memory storage occurs across various regions of the brain, with different types of memory being stored in different areas:

 - **Short-term memory:** Short-term memories are primarily stored in the prefrontal cortex and other cortical regions, where they can be maintained temporarily through sustained neural activity.

 - **Long-term memory:** Long-term memories are distributed throughout the brain, with different types of memories being stored in specific neural networks. The hippocampus plays a large role in the consolidation of new memories, gradually transferring them to more permanent storage sites in the cortex over time.

3. **Retrieval:** Retrieval involves accessing and bringing stored information back into conscious awareness when needed. Retrieval cues, such as context, emotions, or associations, can trigger the activation of memory traces and facilitate retrieval. The process of retrieval can be influenced by various factors, including:

- **Contextual cues:** Memories are often better retrieved in the same or similar context in which they were encoded.

- **Emotional arousal:** Emotionally salient events are often remembered more vividly and retrieved more easily than neutral events.

- **Priming:** Prior exposure to related stimuli can facilitate the retrieval of associated memories through processes such as semantic priming.

Are you still there? Great, I got lost for a minute there thinking about Yersinia Pestis again. Any, what were we talking about? Memory. Yes, yes. Overall, the encoding, storage, and retrieval of memory involve dynamic interactions between various brain regions, chemical reactions, and cognitive processes, shaping our ability to acquire, maintain, and recall information over time.

Memory and Autism

How does memory differ in Autistic people, and how might that impact everyday life for Autistic people?

The research on Autism and memory is still evolving in part because our knowledge of memory is altogether incomplete. Much research into Autistic memory tends to be on children. Perhaps you have noticed that children's brains and adults' brains are different. I have noticed this, too. Adults have a different process of memory. Experience changes the synapses. Both are important because children and adults are also important, and understanding memory differences allows for self-accommodation and appropriate support.

Below are some of the ways in which we know memory differs in Autistic people and how it might impact their everyday lives, but memory still holds some mysteries. I have a great deal of memories I remember in minute, sensory detail like it just happened. I also have times in my life I have hardly any memories at all. More like impressions. One of the strongest memories I have about myself in my Bachelor's degree program is wearing a red trench coat. I have strong memories of other people's stories. That's all to say, I think Autistic and other neurodivergent neurotypes have some memory secrets to share still.

Savantism: A small number of Autistic people—purported to be about 10%, but may be less due to the large volume of undiagnosed Autistics—have unusual and extreme abilities in one or more areas while also having a developmental disability, often Autism.[115] These abilities are often related to reading, math, music, and memory. Because of the fascinating and unusual nature of Savantism, many people have the mistaken belief that all Autistic people have a savant skill.

---

[115] Hughes, J. E., Ward, J., Gruffydd, E., Baron-Cohen, S., Smith, P., Allison, C., & Simner, J. (2018). Savant syndrome has a distinct psychological profile in autism. *Molecular autism*, *9*, 1-18. https://doi.org/10.1186/s13229-018-0237-1

Most Autistic people do not have such skills. But those who do offer those gifts to all and can also teach us a great deal about the human brain. An example of an Autistic with a savant skill is British architectural artist Stephen Wiltshire.[116]

Not only is Wiltshire a skilled artist, but he hand draws cityscapes from memory in accurate detail. One can only speculate as to why he can do this—fly over a city and remember all of its details, but the process of encoding, storage, and retrieval must be happening differently.

Associative memory: Autistics often exhibit a strong **associative memory, which enables them to recall information and make connections between seemingly unrelated concepts.**[117] Associative memory is a type of memory that links new information to something already familiar, making it easier to recall. In Autistic brains, this can manifest as an exceptional ability to remember details, patterns, and relationships. For example, an Autistic person might remember an entire conversation from years ago or recall the exact location of an object they saw months earlier. This strength in associative memory can contribute to

---

[116] Stephen WiltshireMBE, Hon.FSAI, Hon.FSSAA. (2024). Stephen Wiltshire. http://www.stephenwiltshire.co.uk

* [117] Semino, S., Zanobini, M., & Usai, M. C. (2021). Visual memory profile in children with high functioning autism. *Applied Neuropsychology: Child*, 10(1), 26-36. DOI: 10.1080/21622965.2019.1594231

exceptional skills in areas like problem-solving, attention to detail, and learning new information. However, it can also sometimes lead to difficulties with generalization and flexibility because we may rely on these associations and struggle to adapt to new or changing situations.

Visual memory: Many Autistics have exceptional <u>visual memory</u>, **which allows them to recall details and patterns of things they have seen with remarkable accuracy.** They might easily remember the layout of a familiar place, recall specific images or scenes from movies or books, or even reproduce complex designs or artwork with precision. However, the research in this area is contradictory, too, with some studies finding difficulties.[118] Autistics may also rely heavily on visual memory to get through daily tasks, such as recognizing faces (an area we collectively struggle with), remembering objects, and understanding social cues. Tapping into their strong visual memory can sometimes lead to demonstrating the incredible cognitive strengths that come with being Autistic.[119] We may also forget things that we expect to remember.

---

* [118] Salmanian, M., Tehrani-Doost, M., Ghanbari-Motlagh, M., & Shahrivar, Z. (2012). Visual memory of meaningless shapes in children and adolescents with autism spectrum disorders. *Iranian journal of psychiatry*, 7(3), 104–108.

* [119] Soulières, I., Dawson, M., Samson, F., Barbeau, E.B., Sahyoun, C.P., Strangman, G.E., Zeffiro, T.A. and Mottron, L. (2009), Enhanced visual processing contributes to matrix reasoning in autism. Hum. Brain Mapp., 30: 4082-4107. https://doi.org/10.1002/hbm.20831

Declarative memory: Some research finds that declarative memory — memory that includes experiences and information — compensates for other weaknesses.[120]

Autobiographical episodic memory: This is a subset of episodic memory having to do with a person's memories of events that have happened to them.[121] According to contradictory research, Autistics are less likely to reflect on their experiences, infer from them, or recognize patterns in them, OR Autistics are more likely to recall sensory details than social ones.[122] Research largely finds that Autistics have less specific autobiographical memory.[123]

Issues with reflecting on personal experiences could make it difficult to adapt what Autistics have learned when there are changes in context. This is not so much because

---

[120] Ullman MT, Pullman MY. (2015). A compensatory role for declarative memory in neurodevelopmental disorders. Neuroscience of Biobehavior Review Apr;51:205-22. https://doi.org/10.1016/j.neubiorev.2015.01.008

[121] Fivush R. (2011). The development of autobiographical memory. *Annual review of psychology, 62,* 559–582. https://doi.org/10.1146/annurev.psych.121208.131702

[122] Coutelle, R., Goltzene, M. A., Canton, M., Campiglia-Sabourin, M., Rabot, J., Bizet, É., ... & Danion, J. M. (2021). Episodic autobiographical memory in adults with autism spectrum disorder: An exploration with the autobiographical interview. *Frontiers in psychiatry, 11.* https://doi.org/10.3389/fpsyt.2020.593855

[123] Wantzen, P., Boursette, A., Zante, E., Mioche, J., Eustache, F., Guénolé, F., ... & Guillery-Girard, B. (2021). Autobiographical memory and social identity in autism: preliminary results of social positioning and cognitive intervention. *Frontiers in psychology, 12.* https://doi.org/10.3389/fpsyg.2021.641765

Autistic people have weak episodic memory, but because Autistic people tend to use episodic memory as a template for the future, we may not communicate our full experience of a memory in research, so researchers might be making incorrect inferences, and we focus on what is *important* to us.

Episodic memory as a template: What I mean by this is that when Autistic people create autobiographical memories, they are writing a definition of the experience. Children, especially, may struggle to generalize what they have learned through experience because they expect sameness.

We expect the experience labeled "grocery store" to be the same every time. We prepare ourselves for sensory overload, which can spark anxiety. We expect the bananas to be in the same spot in the produce section. We expect self-checkout to be open so we don't have to make small talk. If the experience doesn't match our expectations, determined by memory, we might be more anxious because now we aren't sure what to expect.

This is well illustrated by Gestalt Language Processing (GLP) and research on the topic. In the pioneering research on GLP, Prizant (1983) found that Autistic children created meaningful language through memories of a whole experience, including the specific sensory details.[124] Prizant discusses what I find to be a perfect example of episodic memory and echolalia (the repetition of words and phrases as meaningful speech).

> I returned to visit some young autistic children I had worked with for more than a year but hadn't seen for almost 4 years. One child (who was 5 years old when I worked with him, and 9 years old upon my return visit), began to reproduce segments of conversation that were parts of events which had occurred 4 years earlier. When I asked him if he remembered some of the things we had done, he continued to offer "pieces" of events by recalling segments of dialogue. (Interestingly, some of the dialogue consisted of reproduction of directives and reprimands, a familiar event to parents and teachers).

I don't want to imply that research showing that Autistics lack a strong autobiographical episodic memory is all flawed. I just have questions.

So, while there may be some evidence that Autistics have difficulty making self-references using experiences, my personal experience is that every Autistic person I know reflects on personal experiences far more than neurotypical

---

[124] Prizant, B. M. (1983). Language acquisition and communicative behavior in autism: Toward an understanding of the" whole" of it. *Journal of speech and hearing disorders*, 48(3), 296-307

people, makes inferences about themselves, and finds all manner of patterns. What I see is that people are very focused on how they behave, how others respond, and what that means about themselves. Often, the problem is doing anything about this.

Research methods and communication: The neurotypical expectation is that Autistic people would behave differently if they were able to reflect, infer, and notice patterns, which tend to be skills we possess. Instead, we can only sometimes mask who we are and not actually manufacture different, more typical, brain structures. Perhaps some of the problems in capturing the Autistic experience of memory is in the differences in communication between non-Autistic researchers and Autistic.

What I'm referring to here is an extension of the Double Empathy Problem. The Double Empathy Problem is a theory that while neurotypical people believe that Autistics fail to understand the state of mind, emotions, and empathy, neurotypical people also fail to understand Autistic states of mind, expressions of emotion, and empathy.[125]

---

[125] Milton, D. E. (2012). On the ontological status of autism: The 'double empathy problem'. *Disability & society*, 27(6), 883-887. https://doi.org/10.1080/09687599.2012.710008

For example, one researcher comments in her paper that Autistics rely on "pre-structured narratives over lived, emotional experience."[126] What I read there is that Autistic subjects attempted to relate personal stories using scripts to attempt to ensure the listener understood them. This is one of the ways in which Autistics communicate. I see this as an issue of communication and understanding.

If Autistics aren't being told what is important to the researcher, they will tell the researcher what they think the researcher wants to know in a way they believe they will be understood. That's what happens when you spend all your time being misunderstood. Second to that, Autistics will tell you what they think is important.

Interests may drive what is remembered and what is communicated. Finally, if you have ever spoken to an Autistic person, you will already be aware that Autistics remember and share numerous details of what is important to them. Special interests can dominate Autistic bandwidth. However, studies on memory related to interests are limited in favor of memory studies using standardized tools or situations

---

[126] Brezis, R. S. (2015). Memory integration in the autobiographical narratives of individuals with autism. *Frontiers in Human Neuroscience*, 9, 76. https://doi.org/10.3389/fnhum.2015.00076

devised by the researchers. Additionally, some research indicates what makes sense to me: Autistics may communicate with others more of what is important to them (or more of what was traumatic for them).[127]

Short-term memory/Working memory: Here we are back at the prefrontal cortex and the home of the executive functions. Working memory in Autistics is shown to be reduced when compared to neurotypical people, meaning that Autistic people can have a harder time holding new information in their minds for further processing. We also have a harder time coming up with recent information without getting some cueing.[128]

I can't avoid the impulse to jump in here and tell you that I am the poster child for poor working memory. I can forget anything instantly. I have developed tools for this, but I consistently have to work to not lose information that I don't find fascinating.

Social cognition: Social behaviors are complex and require multiple brain processes, including associating faces and voices to particular contexts, which require robust episodic

---

[127] Li, S. T., Chien, W. C., Chung, C. H., & Tzeng, N. S. (2024). Increased risk of acute stress disorder and post-traumatic stress disorder in children and adolescents with autism spectrum disorder: a nation-wide cohort study in Taiwan. *Frontiers in Psychiatry*, 15. https://doi.org/10.3389/fpsyt.2024.1329836

[128] Desaunay, P., Briant, A. R., Bowler, D. M., Ring, M., Gérardin, P., Baleyte, J. M., ... & Guillery-Girard, B. (2020). Memory in autism spectrum disorder: A meta-analysis of experimental studies. *Psychological Bulletin*, 146(5), 377. https://doi.org/10.1037/bul0000225

memory.[129] There is some speculation in researcher circles that impairments in forming these particular facial associative memory traces could form one of the foundational elements of Autism. Another of those unifying theories that perhaps don't answer all the questions.

Memory of faces: Autistic children have difficulty remembering faces, which can impact social interactions and relationships. This can persist into adulthood when it becomes the condition known as prosopagnosia. This is both a difficulty in recognizing faces and making out emotions on people's faces (Not to be confused with alexithymia, which is difficulty in understanding the emotional state of the self and others).

Metamemory: Research suggests that individuals Autistics have difficulty in evaluating and monitoring their own memory. However, other research finds that difficulties in metamemory are dependent on when the memory task is done, how difficult the task is, and the cues.[130]

---

[129] Banker, S. M., Gu, X., Schiller, D., & Foss-Feig, J. H. (2021). Hippocampal contributions to social and cognitive deficits in autism spectrum disorder. *Trends in neurosciences*, 44(10), 793–807. https://doi.org/10.1016/j.tins.2021.08.005

[130] Wojcik, D. Z., Moulin, C. J., & Souchay, C. (2022). Memory and metamemory for actions in children with autism: Exploring global metacognitive judgements. *Research in Developmental Disabilities*, 124, 104195. https://doi.org/10.1016/j.ridd.2022.104195

Impact on everyday life: Obviously, memory challenges can impact everyday life, including school, work, relationships, and everything in between, from getting the oil changed to making your 3:30 dental checkup.

Memory abilities: Autistic people have some memory skills compared to neurotypical people.
- Autistic people are less likely to remember false information.[131]
- Autistics have enhanced visual memory and short-term visual memory.[132]
- Autistics tend to have good memory skills for facts related to their interests[133] and a declarative memory that compensates for weaknesses in other areas.[134]

---

[131] Beversdorf, D. Q., Smith, B. W., Crucian, G. P., Anderson, J. M., Keillor, J. M., Barrett, A. M., Hughes, J. D., Felopulos, G. J., Bauman, M. L., Nadeau, S. E., & Heilman, K. M. (2000). Increased discrimination of "false memories" in autism spectrum disorder. *Proceedings of the National Academy of Sciences of the United States of America*, 97(15), 8734–8737. https://doi.org/10.1073/pnas.97.15.8734

[132] Nicholls, L. A. B., & Stewart, M. E. (2023). Autistic traits are associated with enhanced working memory capacity for abstract visual stimuli. *Acta Psychologica*, 236, 103905. https://doi.org/10.1016/j.actpsy.2023.103905

[133] Dupuis, A., Mudiyanselage, P., Burton, C. L., Arnold, P. D., Crosbie, J., & Schachar, R. J. (2022). Hyperfocus or flow? Attentional strengths in autism spectrum disorder. *Frontiers in Psychiatry*, 13. https://doi.org/10.3389/fpsyt.2022.886692

[134] Ullman MT, Pullman MY. A compensatory role for declarative memory in neurodevelopmental disorders. Neuroscience Biobehavioral Review Apr;51:205-22. hhtps://doi.org/10.1016/j.neubiorev.2015.01.008

Accommodations and support: There are dozens of ways Autistic people can remind themselves of things, including technology, low-tech methods like writing lists and notes, strewing (leaving visual reminders such as an empty pill bottle to remind you to make a doctor's appointment), and relying on others to aid with reminders. What works for each Autistic person is variable. I find list-making especially helpful, but that isn't helpful to many. I find setting reminders and alarms helpful, but those may just be dismissed and ignored by someone else.

Theories of Memory in Autism

There have been many theories about the brain structure and function that contribute to the differences we see in the memory of Autistic people. However, no one theory appears to account for them all.[135] Several memory models and theories do exist and have something to offer to the conversation:

1. **Monotropism:** Monotropism can explain memory differences in Autism by accounting for strong memory for interests and weak memory for other things.

2. **Atkinson-Shiffrin Model:** This model accounts for different memory stages: sensory, short-term, and long-

---

[135] Cooper, R.A., Simons, J.S. (2019). Exploring the neurocognitive basis of episodic recollection in autism. *Psychology Bulletin(26)* 163–181. https://doi.org/10.3758/s13423-018-1504-z

term.[136] In Autistic people, how sensory information and attention function might affect how they move info from sensory memory to higher memory stages.[137]

3. **Dual Process Theory:** Dual Process Theory distinguishes between automatic, unconscious processes and controlled, conscious processes involved in memory functioning.[138] Autistics may have differences in automatic versus controlled processing, with strengths in certain types of memory tasks (e.g., rote memorization) and challenges in others (e.g., flexible problem-solving).

4. **Associative Learning Theories:** Associative learning theories emphasize the role of associations and connections in memory formation and retrieval. Differences in these processes, such as pattern recognition and contextual integration, may contribute to memory difficulties in Autism, particularly in tasks requiring flexible memory retrieval or generalization, such as predicting outcomes when there are changes.

---

[136] Spielman, R. M., Jenkins, W. J., & Lovett, M. D. (2020). How memory functions. In Psychology 2e. Retrieved from https://openstax.org/details/books/psychology-2e

[137] Pastor-Cerezuela, G., Fernández-Andrés, M. I., Sanz-Cervera, P., & Marín-Suelves, D. (2020). The impact of sensory processing on executive and cognitive functions in children with autism spectrum disorder in the school context. *Research in developmental disabilities*, 96, 103540. https://doi.org/10.1016/j.ridd.2019.103540

[138] Brosnan, M., & Ashwin, C. (2022). Thinking, fast and slow on the autism spectrum. *Autism*. https://doi.org/10.1177/13623613221132437

5. **Weak Central Coherence Theory:** Weak Central Coherence Theory suggests that individuals with ASD may prioritize local processing over global processing, leading to a focus on detail-oriented information processing at the expense of holistic understanding. See chapter two for how I feel about this last part (hint: I disagree). However, memory encoding and retrieval could be impacted by local processing bias.

6. **Mnesic imbalance:** This theory suggests that in Autistics, declarative memory (remembering facts and events) might make up for problems with procedural memory (remembering how to do things).[139] This theory suggests that the imbalance could cause the traits associated with Autism.

Post-Traumatic Stress Disorder (PTSD)

This section <u>will not</u> include any references to specific traumas.

We've already touched on PTSD in Autistic neurotypes when we discussed visual thinking. I'd like to return to the subject here because PTSD is important in the conversation about memory.

---

[139] Vasa, R. A., Mostofsky, S. H., & Ewen, J. B. (2016). The disrupted connectivity hypothesis of autism spectrum disorders: time for the next phase in research. *Biological Psychiatry: Cognitive Neuroscience and Neuroimaging*, 1(3), 245-252. https://doi.org/10.1016/j.bpsc.2016.02.003

Post-Traumatic Stress Disorder is a reaction to traumatic experiences in which the experience is held in the present instead of being processed as a memory. There are many trauma responses that aren't PTSD. People with a history of trauma might avoid situations, see the world differently than they did before, or have mood changes. What makes PTSD different is the set of symptoms known as re-experiencing. **Re-experiencing symptoms are moments when the trauma is happening again in the form of nightmares, intrusive thoughts, flashbacks, and even hallucinations.**

Autistic people are more prone to PTSD. There are two main reasons for this. First is the structure of the brain's connections. Autistic brains have more even connectivity in the hemispheres of the brain while non-Autistic people tend to have more connections on the left side. The corpus callosum is the bridge between the two hemispheres. In Autistics, a thinner bridge allows less traffic.

Second, Autistic people are more likely to be traumatized. The heightened prevalence of traumatic experiences among Autistics can exacerbate existing memory difficulties and further complicate the management of cognitive challenges. In addressing memory interventions and support strategies for this population, it becomes necessary to consider the intersectionality of Autism and PTSD. Tailored interventions should encompass trauma-informed approaches that recognize and address the specific needs and sensitivities of individuals with Autism who have experienced trauma. Environmental modifications and accommodations should be implemented with careful consideration of potential triggers and sensory sensitivities associated with trauma exposure. Practical strategies aimed at enhancing memory functioning should be integrated into trauma-informed care plans, emphasizing personalized approaches that promote resilience and recovery while fostering a supportive and inclusive environment for Autistics affected by PTSD.

I propose a third reason: that our experiences of the world are deeply sensory. I believe the increased likelihood of PTSD in Autistic people can tell us something about memory and emotional processing. So, in addition to differences in memory recall, we have difficulties encoding memory.

Memory Interventions and Support Strategies

Evidence-based interventions and strategies have been extensively explored to enhance memory functioning in individuals with Autism. These interventions aim to address the diverse memory challenges experienced by individuals on the spectrum.

One approach involves tailoring interventions to the specific memory profiles and needs of each individual. By understanding the unique characteristics of an individual's memory difficulties, such as deficits in declarative or procedural memory, interventions can be personalized to target areas of weakness effectively.

Environmental modifications and accommodations may include simplifying instructions, reducing distractions, and providing visual supports to aid memory encoding and retrieval processes. By optimizing the individual's surroundings to align with their cognitive needs, memory difficulties can be mitigated, facilitating better functioning in various settings.

Practical strategies and techniques are implemented across different contexts, including education, employment, and daily living. In educational settings, educators may utilize multi-sensory approaches, repetition, and structured routines to reinforce learning and memory retention. In employment settings, employers may provide job aids, task breakdowns, and organizational tools to support memory-related tasks. In daily living, caregivers and individuals themselves can employ strategies such as creating visual schedules, using memory aids like reminders and checklists, and breaking tasks into manageable steps to enhance memory performance in everyday activities.

Overall, memory interventions and support strategies for individuals with Autism encompass a range of evidence-based approaches tailored to individual needs, environmental modifications to optimize memory performance, and practical strategies implemented across various settings to facilitate better memory functioning and overall quality of life.

Benefits of Memory Differences

Savantism: Approximately 10% of Autistics, though possibly fewer, exhibit exceptional abilities in areas such as memory, reading, math, or music. These savant skills, while not universal among Autistics, can offer unique insights into memory and cognitive processes, contributing to our understanding of the human brain.

Enhanced Visual Memory: Autistics tend to have enhanced visual memory compared to neurotypical individuals. This strength in visual memory can be advantageous in tasks that require remembering visual details or patterns, such as art, design, or certain academic subjects.

Good Memory for Facts Related to Interests: Autistics often have intense, specialized interests, and they tend to have good memory skills for facts related to these interests. This ability to retain detailed information about specific topics can lead to expertise and proficiency in those areas, contributing to innovation and specialization in diverse fields.

Disadvantages of Memory Differences

Working Memory Reduction: Autistics may experience reduced working memory capacity compared to neurotypical individuals. This limitation can make it challenging to hold new information in their minds for further processing, impacting tasks that require multitasking, complex problem-solving, or information retention. *I like to call this "What was I talking about again?"*

Memory of Faces: Autistics, particularly children, may have difficulty remembering faces, which can impair their ability to recognize familiar individuals and interpret social cues accurately. This difficulty may persist into adulthood, affecting relationships and social interactions. *I call this "I will only recognize you if you're 'in the right place.'" If I knew you from work and I saw you at a movie theater, I wouldn't know you. Sorry.*

Metamemory Issues: Research suggests that Autistics may have difficulty evaluating and monitoring their own memory. This can lead to challenges in accurately assessing their memory abilities and employing effective memory strategies, potentially impacting academic or vocational performance. *"I will definitely remember the appointment I just made, which I didn't write down. It's important. NO PROBLEM."*

Impact on Everyday Life: Memory challenges can have significant implications for daily functioning, affecting various aspects of life, including education, employment, relationships, and daily tasks. Difficulties in remembering important information or instructions can lead to frustration, stress, and even cost.

Summary

Memory issues are a part of Autism. The main area of difficulty is working memory, and the main areas of strength are in associative memory and at least some types of visual memory.

Takeaway for Autistics

The takeaway message for Autistics regarding understanding and accommodating their memory issues is twofold: your memory functions with strengths and weaknesses. Play up the strengths and accommodate the weaknesses as you can.

Tips

1. **Self-Awareness and Understanding**: Understand what your memory strengths and weaknesses are. By recognizing areas of difficulty, such as working memory, you can better advocate for yourself and seek appropriate support and accommodations.

2. **Personalized Strategies and Accommodations**: Use technology, create visual aids or schedules, break tasks into

manageable steps, or seek support from others as needed. Experimentation and flexibility are key in finding what methods are most effective in enhancing memory functioning and overall well-being.

Takeaway for those who love or work with Autistics

Memory issues are normal for Autistic people. This is the way the Autistic brain was made. Work with it and provide support without judgment.

Tips

1. **Grace:** Understand that memory isn't the same in Autistic people. Particularly working memory. Autistics may forget something that is fresh in your mind. Give us some grace and some gentle reminders.

2. **Acceptance:** Always. It's going to happen. They will forget some things. It's ok. Make sure they know it's ok.

3. **Support:** Work with the Autistic person to find strategies that actually help and work for them. Reminders, tech, planners, a daily list, or any other usual strategies might work or not. If it takes mental labor to make the support work, it might not be the right fit.

Afterword

Autistic thinking is complex and varied. The heterogeneity of Autism shines through every aspect. While we've learned about the Autistic brain's under- and over-connectivity, Gestalt Cognitive Processing, visual and pattern-based thinking styles, monotropism, executive functions, and memory, there is still <u>so much</u> more to discuss. Things are changing all the time as more and more people learn about their Autistic neurotype. I can't wait to see where we go next.

I hope this book has provided you with some of what you need to understand yourself as an Autistic person better — or to understand the Autistic people in your life if you aren't. The Autistic brain has yet to reveal all of its secrets to science, but **the best way to understand Autism is with kindness and curiosity in relationships with Autistic people.**

My dear reader, your presence through the pages of this book has been scary and *rewarding*. You've been my inspiration and my body double. Every page has included conversations with you. I've tried to anticipate your questions and your speculation. I've enjoyed my time with you immensely. Let's do this again.

Until next time, friends,

Appendices

Appendix 1

A note on language and inclusion from my book *Thriving Together: An Essential Guide to Finding Support and Mastering Self-Care for Caregivers of Children with Differences and Disabilities (2023)*

Identity-first vs. Person-First language

Clears throat How we speak has power, and how we refer to people can be incredibly important to them. How we speak about people can even impact how *we see them*. For this reason, I want to explain my use of language referring to disability.

The person-first language movement, as in "a person with a disability," probably started in Sweden in 1968. A parents' organization for those with disabled adult children used the phrase, "We speak for them," and those disabled adults decided that they would indeed communicate for their own selves. That included being considered people *first* [140]. It was most definitely in play by 1974 when residents of an institution for developmentally disabled people created the organization known as People First. Their inaugural meeting hosted 500 people in attendance and is considered to be the

---

[140] The history of person first language: Crocker, A. F., & Smith, S. N. (2019). Person-first language: are we practicing what we preach?. *Journal of multidisciplinary healthcare*, 12, 125–129. https://doi.org/10.2147/JMDH.S140067

start of the disability self-advocacy movement in the United States[141]. Boss, right?!

Because the world was messed-up back then (in similar and different ways than it is now) people who happened to be disabled were often treated poorly. The nomenclature used to refer to them was so disgusting that we don't even breathe these words today. Advocates decided that one of their primary goals was for people to be treated as though they have autonomy and choice in their lives (as they should). They thought that person-first language would help others see these individuals as people and not as problems or less than others.

Since then, person-first language has been embedded into academic and professional spaces and has been seen as a sacred trust amongst those serving in the medical, mental health, disability, and educational communities. We've also seen person-first language make its way into our everyday vernacular. Person-first language is most likely what you will see in schools, government agencies, and medical environments, though there is some change happening there. The principle behind this is the belief that language can shape perception and person-first humanizes patients into people. The goal is a positive one. However, things are changing, and people and institutions can adapt to those changes.

---

[141] The History of People First: People First. (2022). History of people first. People First, WV. https://www.peoplefirstwv.org/old-front/hidtory-of-people-first/

The identity-first language movement, as in "disabled person," is a current movement that seeks to target ableism (the belief that disabled=bad and non-disabled=good)[142]. The goal is to reduce stigma and honor the humanity of people by accepting and embracing the disabilities or conditions that they consider to be core to their identities. In short, the goal is to say that it's ok to be different, and it doesn't require delicate euphemisms. This movement started in the late 1980s and is still working on gaining broad traction but in some communities such as the Autistic community, it's a big deal because many Autistics see Autism not as an add-on accessory disability but as a natural type of brain, a neurotype.

In the blind and deaf communities, identity-first is used because despite how others may think, blind and deaf people also see being blind or deaf as a part of who they are. Many advocates with physical disabilities use and prefer identity-first. In short, looking around, you will mainly see people who work with or love disabled people call them something other than disabled and disabled people calling themselves disabled, comfortably.

---

[142] Brown, Lydia. (Aug 2011). The significance of semantics: person-first language: why it matters. Autistic Hoya. https://www.autistichoya.com/2011/08/significance-of-semantics-person-first.html

Liebowitz, Cara. (Mar 2015). I am disabled: on identity-first versus people-first language. The body is not an apology. https://thebodyisnotanapology.com/magazine/i-am-disabled-on-identity-first-versus-people-first-language/

American Psychological Association. (Sept 2019). Disability. APA Style Guide. https://apastyle.apa.org/style-grammar-guidelines/bias-free-language/disability

Disability advocates tend to lean towards identity-first, and parents of children and adults tend to prefer euphemisms like "special needs" and person-first language. This is often out of fear of their children being "othered," segregated, and excluded. It's because they are afraid others won't see the child and only the disability. I understand and respect those fears.

What I advocate for is that we see both the person and the disability or the neurology so that we have the whole picture of the person. I have made the conscious decision in this book to use identity-first language to challenge the stigma of disability being something bad, and also just because it makes sense to me that people should get to decide how they want to be addressed and recognized linguistically. I have also included "differences" because some people using the social model of disability don't identify themselves or their children as disabled when they are accommodated. The social model sees disability as only the inability of society to accommodate individuals.

For people in my life and those I meet, I will always respectfully refer to someone the way they wish to be referred to, and I invite you to do the same. This goes for everything! There are communities of people with conditions that prefer person-first, such as those with diabetes or epilepsy. I tried to make the best choices to be inclusive and responsive to the prevailing guidance from disability advocates from the biggest categories of disability.

If this rubs you the wrong way, I understand that and hope you can read on to gain something from this book without distraction. Please know this decision was made with care and love. Please also consider further reading on the topic.

Appendix 2

A word about "functioning labels" and "mental age" from my book *Thriving Together: An Essential Guide to Finding Support and Mastering Self-Care for Caregivers of Children with Differences and Disabilities (2023)*

Functioning labels and mental age terminology are very common in the world of disability and are used mostly by family members and professionals to explain how to orient to the disabled person. Personally and professionally, I do not use functioning labels such as "high functioning" or "low functioning" for multiple reasons. First, they aren't very clear terms with definitions in the diagnostic manuals, so they don't have well-understood meanings; they don't convey much information beyond generalizations. The goal is to tell someone in shorthand what to expect from the disabled person. It's to try to manage the expectations of others, but often what those terms do is place a fence around the person, not of their creation.

A person categorized as "high functioning" having a bad day is expected to behave as a high-functioning person, and when they do not, they can be chastised. A person labeled "low functioning" is chronically underestimated and may not be given access to alternative communication devices, for example, due to the belief that they can't manage to use them. I will not use functioning labels here. I will use the term "high support needs" when necessary, which some people also do not endorse because it can be seen as a euphemism for functioning labels.

I will never use "mental age" here, and I would advocate against using it. Professionals might be wrong about their assessment (it repeatedly happens with my child) because development is non-linear and because it may hurt your child or other disabled people to hear a statement that can be seen as dismissive and even insulting. Using a phrase such as "he's 15 but with the mind of a toddler" might be something told to you by a professional, and it might feel informative when giving it to another person. It may be wrong. If your child lacks a communication method, there is no way to know about their inner life based on outer presentation, actions, and behaviors. I can attest to this in my own experience as a parent.

My 12-year-old is totally non-speaking. Based on her behaviors, we would have no way to know that she's thoughtful, brilliant, sensitive, and pretty damned spicy. This is due to her disability profile. Her school evaluations always include grade levels and an IQ score that reflects only her lack of ability to participate in their tests. Because we have a unique communication method we use while learning a more conventional one, I have conversations with her all day. If they knew what I know, they would be ashamed of the things they have said about her, especially in front of her.

Another issue with mental age is that a person may be advanced in some areas and behind typical peers in others. People don't advance in all areas at the same time—especially disabled and different people.

What of cases of people with significant intellectual disabilities or conditions that impact the body, speech, and movement so that abilities can't be determined? I would say because someone's cognitive skills are not on par with peers and/or they have interests that are more common in children much younger than they are, or these things can't easily be determined, just skip assigning mental age anyway. *The individual is still the age they have lived in their body.* It's important to meet them where they are in all ways, but asking others to assume they are a 2-year-old in a 20-year-old body impacts the way they will be treated, and it probably won't be for the better.

Inclusion

Finally, this book is written for any parent or other caregiver. This includes moms, dads, trans and non-binary people who don't identify with the terms "mom" or "dad," grandparents, step-parents, foster parents, adoptive parents, aunts and uncles, cousins, or anyone else.

The point here is: if you're taking care of kids who have other than the usual childhood support needs, no matter what you or your family look like, you belong here. And thank you for being here.

Printed in Great Britain
by Amazon